Handbook of Digital Marketing

Compiled by
Juliann Moen

Scribbles

Year of Publication 2018

ISBN : 9789387513013

Book Published by

Scribbles

(An Imprint of Alpha Editions)

email - alphaedis@gmail.com

Produced by: PediaPress GmbH
Limburg an der Lahn
Germany
http://pediapress.com/

Contents

Introduction

Digital marketing

<indicator name="pp-default"> 🔒 </indicator>

Digital marketing (also known as **data-driven marketing**) is the marketing of products or services using digital technologies, mainly on the Internet, but also including mobile phones, display advertising, and any other digital medium.

Digital marketing's development since the 1990s and 2000s has changed the way brands and businesses use technology for marketing. As digital platforms are increasingly incorporated into marketing plans and everyday life, and as people use digital devices instead of visiting physical shops, digital marketing campaigns are becoming more prevalent and efficient.

Digital marketing techniques such as search engine optimization (SEO), search engine marketing (SEM), content marketing, influencer marketing, content automation, campaign marketing, data-driven marketing[1] and e-commerce marketing, social media marketing, social media optimization, e-mail direct marketing, display advertising, e–books, and optical disks and games are becoming more common in our advancing technology. In fact, digital marketing now extends to non-Internet channels that provide digital media, such as mobile phones (SMS and MMS), callback, and on-hold mobile ring tones.

History

The term *digital marketing* was first used in the 1990s, but digital marketing has roots in the mid-1980s, when the SoftAd Group, now ChannelNet, developed advertising campaigns for automobile companies: People sent in reader reply cards found in magazines and received in return floppy disks that contained multimedia content promoting various cars and free test drives.Wikipedia:Citation needed

Brandship:
The digital path between brand and consumer

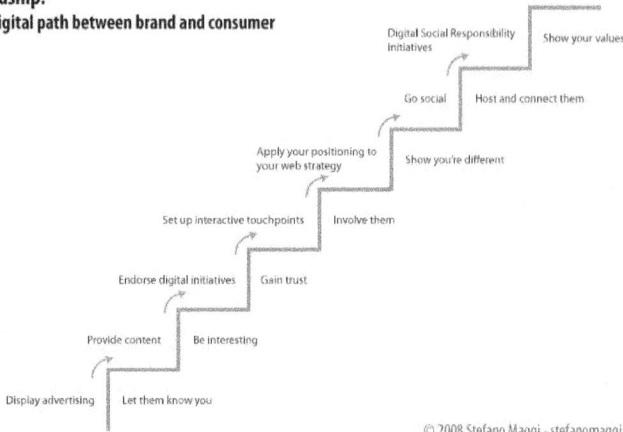

Figure 1: *Certain features of digital marketing that contribute in brand awareness: ease of access and effectiveness*

In 2000 a survey in the United Kingdom found that most retailers had not registered their own domain address.

Digital marketing became more sophisticated in the 2000s and the 2010s, when the proliferation of devices' capability to access digital media at almost any given time led to great growth. Statistics produced in 2012 and 2013 showed that digital marketing was still a growing field.

Digital marketing is often referred to as 'online marketing', 'internet marketing' or 'web marketing'. The term *digital marketing* has grown in popularity over time, particularly in certain countries. In the USA *online marketing* is still prevalent. In Italy, digital marketing is referred to as *web marketing*. In the UK and worldwide, however, *digital marketing* has become the most common term, especially after the year 2013.

Digital media growth is estimated at 4.5 trillion online ads served annually with digital media spend at 48% growth in 2010. An increasing portion of advertising stems from businesses employing Online Behavioural Advertising (OBA) to tailor advertising for internet users, but OBA raises concern of consumer privacy and data protection.

New non-linear marketing approach

In an evermore complex retail environment, customer engagement is essential but challenging. Retailers must shift from a linear marketing approach of one-way communication to a value exchange model of mutual dialogue and benefit-sharing between provider and consumer. Exchanges are more non-linear, free flowing, and both one-to-many or one-on-one. The spread of information and awareness can occur across numerous channels, such as the blogosphere, YouTube, Facebook, Instagram, Snapchat, Pinterest, and a variety of other platforms. Online communities and social networks allow individuals to easily create content and publicly publish their opinions, experiences, and thoughts and feelings about many topics and products, hyper-accelerating the diffusion of information.

The Nielsen Global Connected Commerce Survey conducted interviews in 26 countries to observe how consumers are using the Internet to make shopping decisions in stores and online. Online shoppers are increasingly looking to purchase internationally, with over 50% in the study who purchased online in the last six months stating they bought from an overseas retailer.

Using an omni-channel strategy is becoming increasingly important for enterprises who must adapt to the changing expectations of consumers who want ever-more sophisticated offerings throughout the purchasing journey. Retailers are increasingly focusing on their online presence, including online shops that operate alongside existing store-based outlets. The "endless aisle" within the retail space can lead consumers to purchase products online that fit their needs while retailers do not have to carry the inventory within the physical location of the store. Solely Internet-based retailers are also entering the market; some are establishing corresponding store-based outlets to provide personal services, professional help, and tangible experiences with their products.

An omni-channel approach not only benefits consumers but also benefits business bottom line: Research suggests that customers spend more than double when purchasing through an omni-channel retailer as opposed to a single-channel retailer, and are often more loyal. This could be due to the ease of purchase and the wider availability of products.

Customers are often researching online and then buying in stores and also browsing in stores and then searching for other options online. Online customer research into products is particularly popular for higher-priced items as well as consumable goods like groceries and makeup. Consumers are increasingly using the Internet to look up product information, compare prices, and search for deals and promotions.

Use in the digital era

There are a number of ways brands can use digital marketing to benefit their marketing efforts. The use of digital marketing in the digital era not only allows for brands to market their products and services, but also allows for online customer support through 24/7 services to make customers feel supported and valued. The use of social media interaction allows brands to receive both positive and negative feedback from their customers as well as determining what media platforms work well for them. As such, digital marketing has become an increased advantage for brands and businesses. It is now common for consumers to post feedback online through social media sources, blogs and websites on their experience with a product or brand.[2] It has become increasingly popular for businesses to use and encourage these conversations through their social media channels to have direct contact with the customers and manage the feedback they receive appropriately.

Word of mouth communications and peer-to-peer dialogue often have a greater effect on customers, since they are not sent directly from the company and are therefore not planned. Customers are more likely to trust other customers' experiences. It is increasingly advantageous for companies to use social media platforms to connect with their customers and create these dialogues and discussions. The potential reach of social media is indicated by the fact that in 2015, each month the Facebook app had more than 126 million average unique users and YouTube had over 97 million average unique users.

Brand awareness

Ease of access

A key objective is engaging digital marketing customers and allowing them to interact with the brand through servicing and delivery of digital media. Information is easy to access at a fast rate through the use of digital communications. Users with access to the Internet can use many digital mediums, such as Facebook, YouTube, Forums, and Email etc. Through Digital communications it creates a Multi-communication channel where information can be quickly exchanged around the world by anyone without any regard to whom they are.[3] Social segregation plays no part through social mediums due to lack of face to face communication and information being wide spread instead to a selective audience. This interactive nature allows consumers create conversation in which the targeted audience is able to ask questions about the brand and get familiar with it which traditional forms of Marketing may not offer.[4]

Competitive advantage

By using Internet platforms, businesses can create competitive advantage through various means. To reach the maximum potential of digital marketing, firms use social media as its main tool to create a channel of information. Through this a business can create a system in which they are able to pinpoint behavioral patterns of clients and feedback on their needs. This means of content has shown to have a larger impingement on those who have a long-standing relationship with the firm and with consumers who are relatively active social media users. Relative to this, creating a social media page will further increase relation quality between new consumers and existing consumers as well as consistent brand reinforcement therefore improving brand awareness resulting in a possible rise for consumers up the Brand Awareness Pyramid. Although there may be inconstancy with product images; maintaining a successful social media presence requires a business to be consistent in interactions through creating a two way feed of information; firms consider their content based on the feedback received through this channel, this is a result of the environment being dynamic due to the global nature of the internet. Effective use of digital marketing can result in relatively lowered costs in relation to traditional means of marketing; Lowered external service costs, advertising costs, promotion costs, processing costs, interface design costs and control costs.

Effectiveness

Brand awareness has been proven to work with more effectiveness in countries that are high in uncertainty avoidance, also these countries that have uncertainty avoidance; social media marketing works effectively. Yet brands must be careful not to be excessive on the use of this type of marketing, as well as solely relying on it as it may have implications that could negatively harness their image. Brands that represent themselves in an anthropomorphizing manner are more likely to succeed in situations where a brand is marketing to this demographic. "Since social media use can enhance the knowledge of the brand and thus decrease the uncertainty, it is possible that people with high uncertainty avoidance, such as the French, will particularly appreciate the high social media interaction with an anthropomorphized brand." Moreover, digital platform provides an ease to the brand and its customers to interact directly and exchange their motives virtually.[5]

Latest developments and strategies

One of the major changes that occurred in traditional marketing was the "emergence of digital marketing" (Patrutiu Baltes, Loredana, 2015), this led to the reinvention of marketing strategies in order to adapt to this major change in traditional marketing (Patrutiu Baltes, Loredana, 2015) .

As digital marketing is dependent on technology which is ever-evolving and fast-changing, the same features should be expected from digital marketing developments and strategies. This portion is an attempt to qualify or segregate the notable highlights existing and being used as of press time.Wikipedia:Manual of Style/Dates and numbers#Chronological items

1. **Segmentation**: more focus has been placed on segmentation within digital marketing, in order to target specific markets in both business-to-business and business-to-consumer sectors.
2. **Influencer marketing**: Important nodes are identified within related communities, known as influencers. This is becoming an important concept in digital targeting. It is possible to reach influencers via paid advertising, such as Facebook Advertising or Google Adwords campaigns, or through sophisticated sCRM (social customer relationship management) software, such as SAP C4C, Microsoft Dynamics, Sage CRM and Salesforce CRM. Many universities now focus, at Masters level, on engagement strategies for influencers.

To summarize, Pull digital marketing is characterized by consumers actively seeking marketing content while Push digital marketing occurs when marketers send messages without that content being actively sought by the recipients.

1. **Online behavioural advertising** is the practice of collecting information about a user's online activity over time, "on a particular device and across different, unrelated websites, in order to deliver advertisements tailored to that user's interests and preferences
2. **Collaborative Environment**: A collaborative environment can be set up between the organization, the technology service provider, and the digital agencies to optimize effort, resource sharing, reusability and communications. Additionally, organizations are inviting their customers to help them better understand how to service them. This source of data is called User Generated Content. Much of this is acquired via company websites where the organization invites people to share ideas that are then evaluated by other users of the site. The most popular ideas are evaluated and implemented in some form. Using this method of acquiring data and developing new products can foster the organizations relationship with their customer as well as spawn ideas that would otherwise be overlooked. UGC is low-cost advertising as it is directly from the consumers and can save advertising costs for the organisation.
3. **Data-driven advertising:** Users generate a lot of data in every step they take on the path of customer journey and Brands can now use that data to activate their known audience with data-driven programmatic media

buying. Without exposing customers' privacy, users' Data can be collected from digital channels (e.g.: when customer visits a website, reads an e-mail, or launches and interact with brand's mobile app), brands can also collect data from real world customer interactions, such as brick and mortar stores visits and from CRM and Sales engines datasets. Also known as People-based marketing or addressable media, Data-driven advertising is empowering brands to find their loyal customers in their audience and deliver in real time a much more personal communication, highly relevant to each customers' moment and actions.

An important consideration today while deciding on a strategy is that the digital tools have democratized the promotional landscape.

5. **Remarketing:** Remarketing plays a major role in digital marketing. This tactic allows marketers to publish targeted ads in front of an interest category or a defined audience, generally called searchers in web speak, they have either searched for particular products or services or visited a website for some purpose.

6. **Game advertising**: Game ads are advertisements that exist within computer or video games. One of the most common examples of in-game advertising is billboards appearing in sports games. In-game ads also might appear as brand-name products like guns, cars, or clothing that exist as gaming status symbols.

The new digital era has enabled brands to selectively target their customers that may potentially be interested in their brand or based on previous browsing interests. Businesses can now use social media to select the age range, location, gender and interests of whom they would like their targeted post to be seen by. Furthermore, based on a customer's recent search history they can be 'followed' on the internet so they see advertisements from similar brands, products and services, This allows businesses to target the specific customers that they know and feel will most benefit from their product or service, something that had limited capabilities up until the digital era.

Ways to further increase the effectiveness of digital marketing

A strategy that is linked into the effectiveness of digital marketing is **content marketing**. Content marketing can be briefly described as "delivering the content that your audience is seeking in the places that they are searching for it". It is found that content marketing is highly present in digital marketing and becomes highly successful when content marketing is involved. This is due to content marketing making your brand more relevant to the target consumers, as well as more visible to the target consumer.

Marketers also find email an effective strategy when it comes to digital marketing as it is another way to build a long term relationship with the consumer. Listed below are some aspects that need to be considered to have an effective digital media campaign and aspects that help create an effective email system.

Interesting mail titles differentiate one advertisement from the other. This separates advertisements from the clutter. Differentiation is one factor that can make an advertisement successful in digital marketing because consumers are drawn to it and are more likely to view the advertisement.

Establishment of customer exclusivity: A list of customers and customer's details should be kept on a database for follow up and selected customers can be sent selected offers and promotions of deals related to the customer's previous buyer behaviour. This is effective in digital marketing as it allows organisations to build up loyalty over email.

Low Technical Requirements: In order to get the full use out of digital marketing it is useful to make you advertising campaigns have low technical requirements. This prevents some consumers not being able to understand or view the advertising campaign.

Rewards: The lucrative offers would always help in making your digital campaign a success. Give some reward in the end of the campaign. This would definitely invite more engagement and word of mouth publicity

Ineffective forms of digital marketing

Digital marketing activity is still growing across the world according to the headline global marketing index. Digital media continues to rapidly grow; while the marketing budgets are expanding, traditional media is declining (World Economics, 2015). Digital media helps brands reach consumers to engage with their product or service in a personalised way. Five areas, which are outlined as current industry practices that are often ineffective are prioritizing clicks, balancing search and display, understanding mobiles, targeting, viewability, brand safety and invalid traffic, and cross-platform measurement (Whiteside, 2016). Why these practices are ineffective and some ways around making these aspects effective are discussed surrounding the following points.

Prioritizing clicks

Prioritizing clicks refers to display click ads, although advantageous by being 'simple, fast and inexpensive' rates for display ads in 2016 is only 0.10 percent in the United States. This means one in a thousand click ads are relevant therefore having little effect. This displays that marketing companies should not just use click ads to evaluate the effectiveness of display advertisements (Whiteside, 2016).

Balancing search and display

Balancing search and display for digital display ads are important; marketers tend to look at the last search and attribute all of the effectiveness to this. This then disregards other marketing efforts, which establish brand value within the consumers mind. ComScore determined through drawing on data online, produced by over one hundred multichannel retailers that digital display marketing poses strengths when compared with or positioned alongside, paid search (Whiteside, 2016). This is why it is advised that when someone clicks on a display ad the company opens a landing page, not its home page. A landing page typically has something to draw the customer in to search beyond this page. Things such as free offers that the consumer can obtain through giving the company contact information so that they can use retargeting communication strategies (Square2Marketing, 2012). Commonly marketers see increased sales among people exposed to a search ad. But the fact of how many people you can reach with a display campaign compared to a search campaign should be considered. Multichannel retailers have an increased reach if the display is considered in synergy with search campaigns. Overall both search and display aspects are valued as display campaigns build awareness for the brand so that more people are likely to click on these digital ads when running a search campaign (Whiteside, 2016).

Understanding Mobiles: Understanding mobile devices is a significant aspect of digital marketing because smartphones and tablets are now responsible for 64% of the time US consumers are online (Whiteside, 2016). Apps provide a big opportunity as well as challenge for the marketers because firstly the app needs to be downloaded and secondly the person needs to actually use it. This may be difficult as 'half the time spent on smartphone apps occurs on the individuals single most used app, and almost 85% of their time on the top four rated apps' (Whiteside, 2016). Mobile advertising can assist in achieving a variety of commercial objectives and it is effective due to taking over the entire screen, and voice or status is likely to be considered highly; although the message must not be seen or thought of as intrusive (Whiteside, 2016). Disadvantages of digital media used on mobile devices also include limited creative capabilities, and reach. Although there are many positive aspects including the users entitlement to select product information, digital media creating a flexible message platform and there is potential for direct selling (Belch & Belch, 2012).

Cross-platform measurement: The number of marketing channels continues to expand, as measurement practices are growing in complexity. A cross-platform view must be used to unify audience measurement and media planning. Market researchers need to understand how the Omni-channel affects consumer's behaviour, although when advertisements are on a consumer's device this does not get measured. Significant aspects to cross-platform measurement involves de-duplication and understanding that you have reached an incremental level with another platform, rather than delivering more impressions against people that have previously been reached (Whiteside, 2016). An example is 'ESPN and comScore partnered on Project Blueprint discovering the sports broadcaster achieved a 21% increase in unduplicated daily reach thanks to digital advertising' (Whiteside, 2016). Television and radio industries are the electronic media, which competes with digital and other technological advertising. Yet television advertising is not directly competing with online digital advertising due to being able to cross platform with digital technology. Radio also gains power through cross platforms, in online streaming content. Television and radio continue to persuade and affect the audience, across multiple platforms (Fill, Hughes, & De Franceso, 2013).

Targeting, viewability, brand safety and invalid traffic: Targeting, viewability, brand safety and invalid traffic all are aspects used by marketers to help advocate digital advertising. Cookies are a form of digital advertising, which are tracking tools within desktop devices; causing difficulty, with shortcomings including deletion by web browsers, the inability to sort between multiple users of a device, inaccurate estimates for unique visitors, overstating reach, understanding frequency, problems with ad servers, which cannot distinguish between when cookies have been deleted and when consumers have not previously been exposed to an ad. Due to the inaccuracies influenced by cookies, demographics in the target market are low and vary (Whiteside, 2016). Another element, which is affected within digital marketing, is 'viewabilty' or whether the ad was actually seen by the consumer. Many ads are not seen by a consumer and may never reach the right demographic segment. Brand safety is another issue of whether or not the ad was produced in the context of being unethical or having offensive content. Recognizing fraud when an ad is exposed is another challenge marketers face. This relates to invalid traffic as premium sites are more effective at detecting fraudulent traffic, although non-premium sites are more so the problem (Whiteside, 2016).

Channels

Digital marketing is facilitated by multiple channels, As an advertiser one's core objective is to find channels which result in maximum two-way communication and a better overall ROI for the brand. There are multiple online marketing channels available namely;

- Affiliate marketing - Affiliate marketing is perceived to not be considered a safe, reliable and easy means of marketing through online platform. This is due to a lack of reliability in terms of affiliates that can produce the demanded number of new customers. As a result of this risk and bad affiliates it leaves the brand prone to exploitation in terms of claiming commission that isn't honestly acquired. Legal means may offer some protection against this, yet there are limitations in recovering any losses or investment. Despite this, affiliate marketing allows the brand to market towards smaller publishers, and websites with smaller traffic. Brands that choose to use this marketing often should beware of such risks involved and look to associate with affiliates in which rules are laid down between the parties involved to assure and minimize the risk involved.

- Display advertising - As the term infers, Online Display Advertisement deals with showcasing promotional messages or ideas to the consumer on the internet. This includes a wide range of advertisements like advertising blogs, networks, interstitial ads, contextual data, ads on the search engines, classified or dynamic advertisement etc. The method can target specific audience tuning in from different types of locals to view a particular advertisement, the variations can be found as the most productive element of this method.

- Email marketing - Email marketing in comparison to other forms of digital marketing is considered cheap; it is also a way to rapidly communicate a message such as their value proposition to existing or potential customers. Yet this channel of communication may be perceived by recipients to be bothersome and irritating especially to new or potential customers, therefore the success of email marketing is reliant on the language and visual appeal applied. In terms of visual appeal, there are indications that using graphics/visuals that are relevant to the message which is attempting to be sent, yet less visual graphics to be applied with initial emails are more effective in-turn creating a relatively personal feel to the email. In terms of language, the style is the main factor in determining how captivating the email is. Using casual tone invokes a warmer and gentle and inviting feel to the email in comparison to a formal style. For combinations; it's suggested that to maximize effectiveness; using no graphics/visual alongside casual language. In contrast using no visual appeal and a formal language style is seen as the least effective method.

- Search engine marketing -

- Social Media Marketing - The term 'Digital Marketing' has a number of marketing facets as it supports different channels used in and among these, comes the Social Media. When we use social media channels (Facebook, Twitter, Pinterest, Instagram, Google+, etc.) to market a product or service, the strategy is called Social Media Marketing. It is a procedure wherein strategies are made and executed to draw in traffic for a website or to gain attention of buyers over the web using different social media platforms.

- Social Networking
- Game advertising - In-Game advertising is defined as "inclusion of products or brands within a digital game." The game allows brands or products to place ads within their game, either in a subtle manner or in the form of an advertisement banner. There are many factors that exist in whether brands are successful in their advertising of their brand/product, these being: Type of game, technical platform, 3-D and 4-D technology, game genre, congruity of brand and game, prominence of advertising within the game. Individual factors consist of attitudes towards placement advertisements, game involvement, product involvement, flow or entertainment. The attitude towards the advertising also takes into account not only the message shown but also the attitude towards the game. Dependent of how enjoyable the game is will determine how the brand is perceived, meaning if the game isn't very enjoyable the consumer may subconsciously have a negative attitude towards the brand/product being advertised. In terms of Integrated Marketing Communication "integration of advertising in digital games into the general advertising, communication, and marketing strategy of the firm" is an important as it results in a more clarity about the brand/product and creates a larger overall effect.
- Online PR

1. Video advertising - This type of advertising in terms of digital/online means are advertisements that play on online videos e.g. YouTube videos. This type of marketing has seen an increase in popularity over time. Online Video Advertising usually consists of three types: Pre-Roll advertisements which play before the video is watched, Mid-Roll advertisements which play during the video, or Post-Roll advertisements which play after the video is watched.[6] Post-roll advertisements were shown to have better brand recognition in relation to the other types, where-as "ad-context congruity/incongruity plays an important role in reinforcing ad memorability". Due to selective attention from viewers, there is the likelihood that the message may not be received. The main advantage of video advertising is that it disrupts the viewing experience of the video and therefore there is a difficulty in attempting to avoid them. How a consumer interacts with online video advertising can come down to three stages: Pre attention, attention, and behavioural decision.[7] These online advertisements give the brand/business options and choices. These consist of length, position, adjacent video content which all directly affect the effectiveness of the produced advertisement time, therefore manipulating these variables will yield different results. Length of the advertisement has shown to affect memorability where-as longer duration resulted in increased brand recognition. This type of advertising, due to its nature of interruption of the viewer, it is likely that the consumer may feel as if their

experience is being interrupted or invaded, creating negative perception of the brand. These advertisements are also available to be shared by the viewers, adding to the attractiveness of this platform. Sharing these videos can be equated to the online version of word by mouth marketing, extending number of people reached. Sharing videos creates six different outcomes: these being "pleasure, affection, inclusion, escape, relaxation, and control". As well, videos that have entertainment value are more likely to be shared, yet pleasure is the strongest motivator to pass videos on. Creating a 'viral' trend from mass amount of a brands advertisement can maximize the outcome of an online video advert whether it be positive or a negative outcome.

It is important for a firm to reach out to consumers and create a two-way communication model, as digital marketing allows consumers to give back feed back to the firm on a community based site or straight directly to the firm via email. Firms should seek this long term communication relationship by using multiple forms of channels and using promotional strategies related to their target consumer as well as word-of mouth marketing.

Multi-channel communications

Push and pull message technologies can be used in conjunction.

Self-regulation

The ICC Code has integrated rules that apply to marketing communications using digital interactive media throughout the guidelines. There is also an entirely updated section dealing with issues specific to digital interactive media techniques and platforms. Code self-regulation on use of digital interactive media includes:

- Clear and transparent mechanisms to enable consumers to choose not to have their data collected for advertising or marketing purposes;
- Clear indication that a social network site is commercial and is under the control or influence of a marketer;
- Limits are set so that marketers communicate directly only when there are reasonable grounds to believe that the consumer has an interest in what is being offered;
- Respect for the rules and standards of acceptable commercial behavior in social networks and the posting of marketing messages only when the forum or site has clearly indicated its willingness to receive them;
- Special attention and protection for children.

Advantages and limitations

The whole idea of digital marketing can be a very important aspect in the overall communication between the consumer and the organisation. This is due to digital marketing being able to reach vast numbers of potential consumers at one time.

Another advantage of digital marketing is that consumers are exposed to the brand and the product that is being advertised directly. To clarify the advertisement is easy to access as well it can be accessed any time any place.

However, with digital marketing there are some setbacks to this type of strategy. One major setback that is identified, is that Digital marketing is highly dependent on the internet. This can be considered as a setback because the internet may not be accessible in certain areas or consumers may have poor internet connection.

As well as digital marketing being highly dependent on the Internet is that it is subject to a lot of clutter, so it marketers may find it hard to make their advertisements stand out, as well as get consumers to start conversations about an organisations brand image or products.

As digital marketing continues to grow and develop, brands take great advantage of using technology and the Internet as a successful way to communicate with its clients and allows them to increase the reach of who they can interact with and how they go about doing so,. There are however disadvantages that are not commonly looked into due to how much a business relies on it. It is important for marketers to take into consideration both advantages and disadvantages of digital marketing when considering their marketing strategy and business goals.

An advantage of digital marketing is that the reach is so large that there are no limitations on the geographical reach it can have. This allows companies to become international and expand their customer reach to other countries other than the country it is based or originates from.

As mentioned earlier, technology and the internet allows for 24 hours a day, 7 days a week service for customers as well as enabling them to shop online at any hour of that day or night, not just when the shops are over and across the whole world. This is a huge advantage for retailers to use it and direct customers from the store to its online store. It has also opened up an opportunity for companies to only be online based rather than having an outlet or store due to the popularity and capabilities of digital marketing.

Another advantage is that digital marketing is easy to be measured allowing businesses to know the reach that their marketing is making, whether the digital marketing is working or not and the amount of activity and conversation that is involved.

With brands using the Internet space to reach their target customers; digital marketing has become a beneficial career option as well. At present, companies are more into hiring individuals familiar in implementing digital marketing strategies and this has led the stream to become a preferred choice amongst individuals inspiring institutes to come up and offer professional courses in Digital Marketing.

A disadvantage of digital advertising is the large amount of competing goods and services that are also using the same digital marketing strategies. For example, when someone searches for a specific product from a specific company online, if a similar company uses targeted advertising online then they can appear on the customer's home page, allowing the customer to look at alternative options for a cheaper price or better quality of the same product or a quicker way of finding what they want online.

Some companies can be portrayed by customers negatively as some consumers lack trust online due to the amount of advertising that appears on websites and social media that can be considered frauds. This can affect their image and reputation and make them out to look like a dishonest brand.

Another disadvantage is that even an individual or small group of people can harm image of an established brand. For instance *Dopplegnager* is a term that is used to disapprove an image about a certain brand that is spread by anti-brand activists, bloggers, and opinion leaders. The word *Doppelganger* is a combination of two German words *Doppel* (double) and *Ganger* (walker), thus it means double walker or as in English it is said alter ego. Generally brand creates images for itself to emotionally appeal to their customers. However some would disagree with this image and make alterations to this image and present in funny or cynical way, hence distorting the brand image, hence creating a Doppelganger image, blog or content (Rindfleisch, 2016).

Two other practical limitations can be seen in the case of digital marketing. One,digital marketing is useful for specific categories of products,meaning only consumer goods can be propagated through digital channels.Industrial goods and pharmaceutical products can not be marketed through digital channels. Secondly, digital marketing disseminates only the information to the prospects most of whom do not have the purchasing authority/power. And hence the reflection of digital marketing into real sales volume is skeptical.Wikipedia:Citation needed

Measuring The Effectiveness of Digital Marketing Campaigns

Although the ultimate criteria to evaluate any business initiative should be its return on investment or any other financial metrics in general, the evaluation criteria and metrics for the digital marketing campaigns can be discussed in more details.

The criteria and metrics can be classified according to its type and time span. Regarding the type, we can either evaluate these campaigns "Quantitatively" or "Qualitatively". Quantitative metrics may include "Sales Volume" and "Revenue Increase/Decrease". While qualitative metrics may include the enhanced "Brand awareness, image and health" as well as the "relationship with the customers".

Shifting the focus to the time span, we may need to measure some "Interim Metrics", which give us some insight during the journey itself, as well as we need to measure some "Final Metrics" at the end of the journey to inform use if the overall initiative was successful or not. As an example, most of social media metrics and indicators such as likes, shares and engagement comments may be classified as interim metrics while the final increase/decrease in sales volume is clearly from the final category.

Of course, the correlation between these categories should exist. Otherwise, a disappointing results may happen at the end in-spite of the illusion of success perceived early during the project.

Digital Marketing Strategy

Planning

Digital marketing system

Digital marketing planning is a term used in marketing management. It describes the first stage of forming a digital marketing strategy for the wider digital marketing system. The difference between digital and traditional marketing planning is that it uses digitally based communication tools and technology such as Social, Web, Mobile, Scannable Surface. Nevertheless, both are aligned with the vision, the mission of the company and the overarching business strategy.

Stages of planning

Using Dr Dave Chaffey's approach, the Digital Marketing Planning (DMP) has three main stages; Opportunity, Strategy and Action. He Suggests that any business looking to implement a successful digital marketing strategy must structure their plan by looking at opportunity, strategy and action. This generic strategic approach often has phases of situation review, goal setting, strategy formulation, resource allocation and monitoring.

1) Opportunity

To create an effective DMP a business first needs to review the marketplace and set 'SMART' (Specific, Measurable, Actionable, Relevant and Time-Bound) objectives.[8] They can set SMART objectives by reviewing the current benchmarks and Key Performance Indicators (KPIs) of the company and competitors. It is pertinent that the analytics used for the KPIs be customised to the type, objectives, mission and vision of the company.,[9,10]

Companies can scan for marketing and sales opportunities by reviewing their own outreach as well as influencer outreach. This means they have competitive advantage because they are able to analyse their co-marketers influence and brand associations.[11]

To cease opportunity, the firm should summarize their current customers' personas and purchase journey from this they are able to deduce their digital marketing capability. This means they need to form a clear picture of where they are currently and how many resources they can allocate for their digital marketing strategy i.e. labour, time etc. By summarizing the purchase journey, they can also recognise gaps and growth for future marketing opportunities that will either meet objectives or propose new objectives and increase profit.

2) Strategy

To create a planned digital strategy, the company must review their digital proposition (what you are offering to consumers) and communicate it using digital customer targeting techniques. So, they must define online value proposition (OVP), this means the company must express clearly what they are offering customers online e.g. brand positioning.

The company should also (re)select target market segments and personas and define digital targeting approaches.

After doing this effectively, it is important to review the marketing mix for online options. The marketing mix comprises the 4Ps - Product, Price, Promotion and Place.[12,13] Some academics have added three additional elements to the traditional 4Ps of marketing Process, Place and Physical appearance making it 7Ps of marketing.[14]

3) Action

The third and final stage requires the firm to set a budget and management systems; these must be measurable touchpoints such as audience reach across all digital platforms. Furthermore, marketers must ensure the budget and management systems are integrating the paid, owned and earned media of the company.[15] The Action and final stage of planning also requires the company to set in place measurable content creation e.g. oral, visual or written online media.[16]

After confirming the digital marketing plan, a scheduled format of digital communications e.g. Gantt Chart should be encoded throughout the internal operations of the company. This ensures that all platforms used fall in line and complement each other for the succeeding stages of digital marketing strategy.

Further reading

- Ryan, Damian; Jones, Calvin (2009), *Understanding digital marketing: marketing strategies for engaging the digital generation*, Kogan Page, ISBN 0749453893
- Carter, Ben; Brooks, Gregory; Catalano, Frank; Smith, Bud (2007), *Digital Marketing for Dummies*, John Wiley & Sons, ISBN 9780470057933

Channels

Affiliate marketing

<indicator name="pp-default"> 🔒 </indicator>

Part of a series on
Internet marketing
• Search engine optimization   • Local search engine optimisation   • Social media marketing   • Email marketing   • Referral marketing   • Content marketing   • Native advertising
Search engine marketing
• Pay-per-click   • Cost per impression   • Search analytics   • Web analytics
Display advertising
• Ad blocking   • Contextual advertising   • Behavioral targeting
Affiliate marketing
• Cost per action   • Revenue sharing
Mobile advertising
• $\frac{v}{t}$ • $\frac{}{e}^{17}$

Affiliate marketing is a type of performance-based marketing in which a business rewards one or more affiliates for each visitor or customer brought by the affiliate's own marketing efforts. The industry has four core players: the merchant (also known as 'retailer' or 'brand'), the network (that contains offers for the affiliate to choose from and also takes care of the payments), the publisher (also known as 'the affiliate'), and the customer. The market has grown in complexity, resulting in the emergence of a secondary tier of players, including affiliate management agencies, super-affiliates and specialized third party vendors.

Affiliate marketing overlaps with other Internet marketing methods to some degree, because affiliates often use regular advertising methods. Those methods include organic search engine optimization (SEO), paid search engine marketing (PPC – Pay Per Click), e-mail marketing, content marketing and in some sense display advertising. On the other hand, affiliates sometimes use less orthodox techniques, such as publishing reviews of products or services offered by a partner.

Affiliate marketing is commonly confused with referral marketing, as both forms of marketing use third parties to drive sales to the retailer. However, both are distinct forms of marketing and the main difference between them is that affiliate marketing relies purely on financial motivations to drive sales while referral marketing relies on trust and personal relationships to drive sales.

Affiliate marketing is frequently overlooked by advertisers.[18] While search engines, e-mail, and website syndication capture much of the attention of online retailers, affiliate marketing carries a much lower profile. Still, affiliates continue to play a significant role in e-retailers' marketing strategies.

History

Origin

The concept of revenue sharing—paying commission for referred business—predates affiliate marketing and the Internet. The translation of the revenue share principles to mainstream e-commerce happened in November 1994, almost four years after the origination of the World Wide Web.

The concept of affiliate marketing on the Internet was conceived of, put into practice and patented by William J. Tobin, the founder of PC Flowers & Gifts. Launched on the Prodigy Network in 1989, PC Flowers & Gifts remained on the service until 1996. By 1993, PC Flowers & Gifts generated sales in excess of $6 million per year on the Prodigy service. In 1998, PC Flowers and Gifts developed the business model of paying a commission on sales to the Prodigy Network.[19,20]

In 1994, Tobin launched a beta version of PC Flowers & Gifts on the Internet in cooperation with IBM, who owned half of Prodigy.[21] By 1995 PC Flowers & Gifts had launched a commercial version of the website and had 2,600 affiliate marketing partners on the World Wide Web. Tobin applied for a patent on tracking and affiliate marketing on January 22, 1996, and was issued U.S. Patent number 6,141,666 on Oct 31, 2000. Tobin also received Japanese Patent number 4021941 on Oct 5, 2007, and U.S. Patent number 7,505,913 on Mar 17, 2009, for affiliate marketing and tracking.[22] In July 1998 PC Flowers and Gifts merged with Fingerhut and Federated Department Stores.[23]

Cybererotica was among the early innovators in affiliate marketing with a cost per click program.[24]

In November 1994, CDNow launched its BuyWeb program. CDNow had the idea that music-oriented websites could review or list albums on their pages that their visitors might be interested in purchasing. These websites could also offer a link that would take visitors directly to CDNow to purchase the albums. The idea for remote purchasing originally arose from conversations with music label Geffen Records in the fall of 1994. The management at Geffen wanted to sell its artists' CD's directly from its website, but did not want to implement this capability itself. Geffen asked CDNow if it could design a program where CDNow would handle the order fulfillment. Geffen realized that CDNow could link directly from the artist on its website to Geffen's website, bypassing the CDNow home page and going directly to an artist's music page.[25]

Amazon.com (Amazon) launched its associate program in July 1996: Amazon associates could place banner or text links on their site for individual books, or link directly to the Amazon home page.

When visitors clicked from the associate's website to Amazon and purchased a book, the associate received a commission. Amazon was not the first merchant to offer an affiliate program, but its program was the first to become widely known and serve as a model for subsequent programs.[26,27]

In February 2000, Amazon announced that it had been granted a patent on components of an affiliate program. The patent application was submitted in June 1997, which predates most affiliate programs, but not PC Flowers & Gifts.com (October 1994), AutoWeb.com (October 1995), Kbkids.com/BrainPlay.com (January 1996), EPage (April 1996), and several others.

Historic development

Affiliate marketing has grown quickly since its inception. The e-commerce website, viewed as a marketing toy in the early days of the Internet, became an integrated part of the overall business plan and in some cases grew to a bigger business than the existing offline business. According to one report, the total sales amount generated through affiliate networks in 2006 was £2.16 billion in the United Kingdom alone. The estimates were £1.35 billion in sales in 2005.[28] MarketingSherpa's research team estimated that, in 2006, affiliates worldwide earned US$6.5 billion in bounty and commissions from a variety of sources in retail, personal finance, gaming and gambling, travel, telecom, education, publishing, and forms of lead generation other than contextual advertising programs.[29]

In 2006, the most active sectors for affiliate marketing were the adult gambling, retail industries and file-sharing services.:149–150 The three sectors expected to experience the greatest growth are the mobile phone, finance, and travel sectors. Soon after these sectors came the entertainment (particularly gaming) and Internet-related services (particularly broadband) sectors. Also several of the affiliate solution providers expect to see increased interest from business-to-business marketers and advertisers in using affiliate marketing as part of their mix.:149–150

Web 2.0

Websites and services based on Web 2.0 concepts—blogging and interactive online communities, for example—have impacted the affiliate marketing world as well. These platforms allow improved communication between merchants and affiliates. Web 2.0 platforms have also opened affiliate marketing channels to personal bloggers, writers, and independent website owners. Contextual ads allow publishers with lower levels of web traffic to place affiliate ads on websites.Wikipedia:Citation needed

Forms of new media have also diversified how companies, brands, and ad networks serve ads to visitors. For instance, YouTube allows video-makers to embed advertisements through Google's affiliate network. New developments have made it more difficult for unscrupulous affiliates to make money. Emerging black sheep are detected and made known to the affiliate marketing community with much greater speed and efficiency. Wikipedia:Citation needed

Compensation methods

Predominant compensation methods

Eighty percent of affiliate programs today use revenue sharing or pay per sale (PPS) as a compensation method, nineteen percent use cost per action (CPA), and the remaining programs use other methods such as cost per click (CPC) or cost per mille (CPM, cost per estimated 1000 views).Wikipedia:Citation needed

Diminished compensation methods

Within more mature markets, less than one percent of traditional affiliate marketing programs today use cost per click and cost per mille. However, these compensation methods are used heavily in display advertising and paid search.

Cost per mille requires only that the publisher make the advertising available on his or her website and display it to the page visitors in order to receive a commission. Pay per click requires one additional step in the conversion process to generate revenue for the publisher: A visitor must not only be made aware of the advertisement, but must also click on the advertisement to visit the advertiser's website.

Cost per click was more common in the early days of affiliate marketing, but has diminished in use over time due to click fraud issues very similar to the click fraud issues modern search engines are facing today. Contextual advertising programs are not considered in the statistic pertaining to diminished use of cost per click, as it is uncertain if contextual advertising can be considered affiliate marketing.

While these models have diminished in mature e-commerce and online advertising markets they are still prevalent in some more nascent industries. China is one example where Affiliate Marketing does not overtly resemble the same model in the West. With many affiliates being paid a flat "Cost Per Day" with some networks offering Cost Per Click or CPM.

Performance/Affiliate marketing

In the case of cost per mille/click, the publisher is not concerned about a visitor being a member of the audience that the advertiser tries to attract and is able to convert, because at this point the publisher has already earned his commission. This leaves the greater, and, in case of cost per mille, the full risk and loss (if the visitor can not be converted) to the advertiser.

Cost per action/sale methods require that referred visitors do more than visit the advertiser's website before the affiliate receives commission. The advertiser must convert that visitor first. It is in the best interest for the affiliate to send the most closely targeted traffic to the advertiser as possible to increase the chance of a conversion. The risk and loss is shared between the affiliate and the advertiser.

Affiliate marketing is also called "performance marketing", in reference to how sales employees are typically being compensated. Such employees are typically paid a commission for each sale they close, and sometimes are paid performance incentives for exceeding objectives.[30] Affiliates are not employed by the advertiser whose products or services they promote, but the compensation models applied to affiliate marketing are very similar to the ones used for people in the advertisers' internal sales department.

The phrase, "Affiliates are an extended sales force for your business", which is often used to explain affiliate marketing, is not completely accurate. The primary difference between the two is that affiliate marketers provide little if any influence on a possible prospect in the conversion process once that prospect is directed to the advertiser's website. The sales team of the advertiser, however, does have the control and influence up to the point where the prospect signs the contract or completes the purchase.

Multi-tier programs

Some advertisers offer multi-tier programs that distribute commission into a hierarchical referral network of sign-ups and sub-partners. In practical terms, publisher "A" signs up to the program with an advertiser and gets rewarded for the agreed activity conducted by a referred visitor. If publisher "A" attracts publishers "B" and "C" to sign up for the same program using his sign-up code, all future activities performed by publishers "B" and "C" will result in additional commission (at a lower rate) for publisher "A".

Two-tier programs exist in the minority of affiliate programs; most are simply one-tier. Referral programs beyond two-tier resemble multi-level marketing (MLM) or network marketing but are different: Multi-level marketing (MLM) or network marketing associations tend to have more complex commission requirements/qualifications than standard affiliate programs.Wikipedia:Citation needed

From the advertiser's perspective

Advantages for merchants

Merchants favor affiliate marketing because in most cases it uses a "pay for performance" model, meaning that the merchant does not incur a marketing expense unless results are accrued (excluding any initial setup cost).[31]

Implementation options

Some merchants run their own (in-house) affiliate programs using dedicated software, while others use third-party intermediaries to track traffic or sales that are referred from affiliates. There are two different types of affiliate management methods used by merchants: standalone software or hosted services, typically called affiliate networks. Payouts to affiliates or publishers can be made by the networks on behalf of the merchant, by the network, consolidated across all merchants where the publisher has a relationship with and earned commissions or directly by the merchant itself.

Affiliate management and program management outsourcing

Uncontrolled affiliate programs aid rogue affiliates, who use spamming,[32] trademark infringement, false advertising, cookie stuffing, typosquatting,[33] and other unethical methods that have given affiliate marketing a negative reputation.

Some merchants are using outsourced (affiliate) program management (OPM) companies, which are themselves often run by affiliate managers and network program managers.[34] OPM companies perform affiliate program management for the merchants as a service, similar to the role an advertising agencies serves in offline marketing.

Types of affiliate websites

Affiliate websites are often categorized by merchants (advertisers) and affiliate networks. There are currently no industry-wide standards for the categorization. The following types of websites are generic, yet are commonly understood and used by affiliate marketers.

- Search affiliates that utilize pay per click search engines to promote the advertisers' offers (i.e., search arbitrage)
- Price comparison service websites and directories
- Loyalty websites, typically characterized by providing a reward or incentive system for purchases via points, miles, cash back
- Cause Related Marketing sites that offer charitable donations

- Coupon and rebate websites that focus on sales promotions
- Content and niche market websites, including product review sites
- Personal websites
- Weblogs and websites syndication feeds
- E-mail marketing list affiliates (i.e., owners of large opt-in -mail lists that typically employ e-mail drip marketing) and newsletter list affiliates, which are typically more content-heavy
- Registration[35] path or co-registration affiliates who include offers from other merchants during the registration process on their own website
- Shopping directories that list merchants by categories without providing coupons, price comparisons, or other features based on information that changes frequently, thus requiring continual updates
- Cost per action networks (i.e., top-tier affiliates) that expose offers from the advertiser with which they are affiliated to their own network of affiliates
- Websites using adbars (e.g. AdSense) to display context-sensitive advertising for products on the site
- Virtual currency that offers advertising views in exchange for a handout of virtual currency in a game or other virtual platform.
- File-Sharing: Web sites that host directories of music, movies, games and other software. Users upload content to file-hosting sites, and then post descriptions of the material and their download links on directory sites. Uploaders are paid by the file-hosting sites based on the number of times their files are downloaded. The file-hosting sites sell premium download access to the files to the general public. The web sites that host the directory services sell advertising and do not host the files themselves.
- Video sharing websites: YouTube videos are often utilized by affiliates to do affiliate marketing. A person would create a video and place a link to the affiliate product they are promoting in the video itself and within the description.

Publisher recruitment

Affiliate networks that already have several advertisers typically also have a large pool of publishers. These publishers could be potentially recruited, and there is also an increased chance that publishers in the network apply to the program on their own, without the need for recruitment efforts by the advertiser.

Relevant websites that attract the same target audiences as the advertiser but without competing with it are potential affiliate partners as well. Vendors or existing customers can also become recruits if doing so makes sense and does not violate any laws or regulations (such as with pyramid schemes).

Almost any website could be recruited as an affiliate publisher, but high I traffic websites are more likely interested in (for their sake) low-risk cost per mille or medium-risk cost per click deals rather than higher-risk cost per action or revenue share deals.[36]

Locating affiliate programs

There are three primary ways to locate affiliate programs for a target website:

1. Affiliate program directories,
2. Large affiliate networks that provide the platform for dozens or even hundreds of advertisers, and
3. The target website itself. (Websites that offer an affiliate program often have a link titled "affiliate program", "affiliates", "referral program", or "webmasters"—usually in the footer or "About" section of the website.)

If the above locations do not yield information pertaining to affiliates, it may be the case that there exists a non-public affiliate program. Utilizing one of the common website correlation methods may provide clues about the affiliate network. The most definitive method for finding this information is to contact the website owner directly, if a contact method can be located.

Past and current issues

Since the emergence of affiliate marketing, there has been little control over affiliate activity. Unscrupulous affiliates have used spam, false advertising, forced clicks (to get tracking cookies set on users' computers), adware, and other methods to drive traffic to their sponsors. Although many affiliate programs have terms of service that contain rules against spam, this marketing method has historically proven to attract abuse from spammers.

E-mail spam

In the infancy of affiliate marketing, many Internet users held negative opinions due to the tendency of affiliates to use spam to promote the programs in which they were enrolled.[37] As affiliate marketing matured, many affiliate merchants have refined their terms and conditions to prohibit affiliates from spamming.

Search engine spam

As search engines have become more prominent, some affiliate marketers have shifted from sending e-mail spam to creating automatically generated webpages that often contain product data feeds provided by merchants. The goal of such webpages is to manipulate the relevancy or prominence of resources indexed by a search engine, also known as *spamdexing*. Each page can be targeted to a different niche market through the use of specific keywords, with the result being a skewed form of search engine optimization.

Spam is the biggest threat to organic search engines, whose goal is to provide quality search results for keywords or phrases entered by their users. Google's PageRank algorithm update ("BigDaddy") in February 2006—the final stage of Google's major update ("Jagger") that began in mid-summer 2005—specifically targeted spamdexing with great success. This update thus enabled Google to remove a large amount of mostly computer-generated duplicate content from its index.[38]

Websites consisting mostly of affiliate links have previously held a negative reputation for underdelivering quality content. In 2005 there were active changes made by Google, where certain websites were labeled as "thin affiliates".[39] Such websites were either removed from Google's index or were relocated within the results page (i.e., moved from the top-most results to a lower position). To avoid this categorization, affiliate marketer webmasters must create quality content on their websites that distinguishes their work from the work of spammers or banner farms, which only contain links leading to merchant sites.

Some commentators originally suggested that affiliate links work best in the context of the information contained within the website itself. For instance, if a website contains information pertaining to publishing a website, an affiliate link leading to a merchant's internet service provider (ISP) within that website's content would be appropriate. If a website contains information pertaining to sports, an affiliate link leading to a sporting goods website may work well within the context of the articles and information about sports. The goal in this case is to publish quality information within the website and provide context-oriented links to related merchant's websites.

However, more recent examples exist of "thin" affiliate sites that are using the affiliate marketing model to create value for Consumers by offering them a service. These thin content service Affiliate fall into three categories:

- Price comparison
- Cause related marketing
- Time saving

Consumer countermeasures

The implementation of affiliate marketing on the internet relies heavily on various techniques built into the design of many web-pages and web-sites, and the use of calls to external domains to track user actions (click tracking, Ad Sense) and to serve up content (advertising) to the user. Most of this activity adds time Wikipedia:Citation needed and is generally a nuisance to the casual web-surfer and is seen as visual clutter. Wikipedia:Citation needed Various countermeasures have evolved over time to prevent or eliminate the appearance of advertising when a web-page is rendered. Third party programs (Ad-Aware, Adblock Plus, Spybot, pop-up blockers, etc.) and particularly, the use of a comprehensive HOSTS file can effectively eliminate the visual clutter and the extra time and bandwidth needed to render many web pages. The use of specific entries in the HOSTS file to block these well-known and persistent marketing and click-tracking domains can also aid in reducing a system's exposure to malware by preventing the content of infected advertising or tracking servers to reach a user's web-browser. Wikipedia:Citation needed

Adware

Although it differs from spyware, adware often uses the same methods and technologies. Merchants initially were uninformed about adware, what impact it had, and how it could damage their brands. Affiliate marketers became aware of the issue much more quickly, especially because they noticed that adware often overwrites tracking cookies, thus resulting in a decline of commissions. Affiliates not employing adware felt that it was stealing commission from them. Adware often has no valuable purpose and rarely provides any useful content to the user, who is typically unaware that such software is installed on his/her computer.

Affiliates discussed the issues in Internet forums and began to organize their efforts. They believed that the best way to address the problem was to discourage merchants from advertising via adware. Merchants that were either indifferent to or supportive of adware were exposed by affiliates, thus damaging those merchants' reputations and tarnishing their affiliate marketing efforts. Many affiliates either terminated the use of such merchants or switched to a competitor's affiliate program. Eventually, affiliate networks were also forced by merchants and affiliates to take a stand and ban certain adware publishers from their network. The result was Code of Conduct by Commission Junction/beFree and Performics,[40] LinkShare's Anti-Predatory Advertising Addendum,[41] and ShareASale's complete ban of software applications as a medium for affiliates to promote advertiser offers.[42] Regardless of the progress made, adware continues to be an issue, as demonstrated by the class action lawsuit against ValueClick and its daughter company Commission Junction filed on April 20, 2007.[43]

Trademark bidding

Affiliates were among the earliest adopters of pay per click advertising when the first pay-per-click search engines emerged during the end of the 1990s. Later in 2000 Google launched its pay per click service, Google AdWords, which is responsible for the widespread use and acceptance of pay per click as an advertising channel. An increasing number of merchants engaged in pay per click advertising, either directly or via a search marketing agency, and realized that this space was already occupied by their affiliates. Although this situation alone created advertising channel conflicts and debates between advertisers and affiliates, the largest issue concerned affiliates bidding on advertisers names, brands, and trademarks. Several advertisers began to adjust their affiliate program terms to prohibit their affiliates from bidding on those type of keywords. Some advertisers, however, did and still do embrace this behavior, going so far as to allow, or even encourage, affiliates to bid on any term, including the advertiser's trademarks.

Compensation disclosure

Bloggers and other publishers may not be aware of disclosure guidelines set forth by the FTC. Guidelines affect celebrity endorsements, advertising language, and blogger compensation.[44]

Lack of industry standards

Certification and training

Affiliate marketing currently lacks industry standards for training and certification. There are some training courses and seminars that result in certifications; however, the acceptance of such certifications is mostly due to the reputation of the individual or company issuing the certification. Affiliate marketing is not commonly taught in universities, and only a few college instructors work with Internet marketers to introduce the subject to students majoring in marketing.[45]

Education occurs most often in "real life" by becoming involved and learning the details as time progresses. Although there are several books on the topic, some so-called "how-to" or "silver bullet" books instruct readers to manipulate holes in the Google algorithm, which can quickly become out of date, or suggest strategies no longer endorsed or permitted by advertisers.[46]

Outsourced Program Management companies typically combine formal and informal training, providing much of their training through group collaboration and brainstorming. Such companies also try to send each marketing employee to the industry conference of their choice.[47]

Other training resources used include online forums, weblogs, podcasts, video seminars, and specialty websites.

Code of conduct

A code of conduct was released by affiliate networks Commission Junction/beFree and Performics in December 2002 to guide practices and adherence to ethical standards for online advertising.

Marketing term

Members of the marketing industry are recommending that "affiliate marketing" be substituted with an alternative name.[48] Affiliate marketing is often confused with either network marketing or multi-level marketing. *Performance marketing* is a common alternative, but other recommendations have been made as well.Wikipedia:Citation needed

Sales tax vulnerability

In April 2008 the State of New York inserted an item in the state budget asserting sales tax jurisdiction over Amazon.com sales to residents of New York, based on the existence of affiliate links from New York–based websites to Amazon.[49] The state asserts that even one such affiliate constitutes Amazon having a business presence in the state, and is sufficient to allow New York to tax all Amazon sales to state residents. Amazon challenged the amendment and lost at the trial level in January, 2009. The case is currently making its way through the New York appeals courts.

Cookie stuffing

Cookie stuffing involves placing an affiliate tracking cookie on a website visitor's computer without their knowledge, which will then generate revenue for the person doing the cookie stuffing. This not only generates fraudulent affiliate sales, but also has the potential to overwrite other affiliates' cookies, essentially stealing their legitimately earned commissions.

Click to reveal

Many voucher code web sites use a click-to-reveal format, which requires the web site user to click to reveal the voucher code. The action of clicking places the cookie on the website visitor's computer. In the United Kingdom, the IAB Affiliate Council under chair Matt Bailey announced regulations[50] that stated that "Affiliates must not use a mechanism whereby users are encouraged to click to interact with content where it is unclear or confusing what the outcome will be."

External links

* Affiliate marketing[51] at DMOZ
* Affiliate Programs[52] at the BOTW Directory

Display advertising

Part of a series on **Internet marketing**
• Search engine optimization • Local search engine optimisation • Social media marketing • Email marketing • Referral marketing • Content marketing • Native advertising
Search engine marketing
• Pay-per-click • Cost per impression • Search analytics • Web analytics
Display advertising
• Ad blocking • Contextual advertising • Behavioral targeting
Affiliate marketing
• Cost per action • Revenue sharing
Mobile advertising
• v • $\underline{t}$ • $\underline{e}$.53

Display advertising is advertising on websites. It includes many different formats and contains items such as text, images, flash, video, and audio. The main purpose of display advertising is to deliver general advertisements and brand messages to site visitors.

According to eMarketer, Facebook and Twitter will take 33% of display ad spending market share by 2017. Also, desktop display advertising has eclipsed search ad buying in 2014, with mobile ad spending to overtake display in 2015.

The example of display advertising

Marketing campaign by display advertising

Display advertising is an online form of advertising that the company's promotional messages appear on third party sites or search engine results pages such as publishers or social networks. The main purpose of display advertising is to support a brand awareness (Robinson et al., 2007).[54] and it also helps to increase a purchase intention of consumers.

Nowadays, social media has been used in many organizations, in particular, ASOS is an online clothing retailer has used social media in its campaign in term of advertising and promoting its products. In 2014, ASOS and Nike co-operated with Google Hangout to create the first shoppable video web chat on Google+. The video is an example of display advertising used for celebrating 27 years of Nike's Air Max trainers. The video advertising aimed at creating brand awareness among users and convincing them to watch the Hangout and purchase products from the display advertising itself. Consumers were able to shop directly from the display advertising. According to ASOS plc statement, display advertising has contributed to the increasing number of users visiting to the website and the rising of downloading ASOS application by 28 per cent of online users. Additionally, the users have visited the website eight times a month on average.[55]

History

Since the early 1990s, the advent of the Internet has completely changed the way people relate to advertisements. As computers prices decreased, online content became accessible to a large portion of the world's population. This change has modified the way people are exposed to media and advertising and has led to the creation of online channels through which advertisements can reach users.

The first type of relationship between a website and an advertiser was a straightforward, direct partnership. This partnership model implies that the advertiser promoting a product or service pays the website (also known as a publisher) directly for a certain amount of ad impressions. As time went on, publishers began creating thousands of websites, leading to millions of pages with unsold ad space. This gave rise to a new set of companies called Ad Networks. The ad network acted as a broker, buying unsold ad space from multiple publishers and packaged them into audiences to be sold to advertisers. This second wave of advertiser-publisher relationships rapidly gained popularity as it was convenient and useful for buyers who often found themselves paying a lower price yet receiving enhanced targeting capabilities through ad networks.

The third and most recent major development that shaped the advertiser-publisher ecosystem started occurring in the late 2000s when widespread adoption of RTB (real time bidding) technology took place. Also referred to as programmatic bidding, RTB allowed companies representing buyers and sellers to bid on the price to show an ad to a user every time a banner ad is loading. When a page loads during a user visit, there are thousands of bids occurring from advertisers to serve an ad to that user, based on each company's individual algorithms. With this most recent change in the industry, more and more ads are being sold on a single-impression basis, as opposed to in bulk purchases.

First online advertisement

The birthday of the first banner display on the World Wide Web was on the 27th October 1994. It appeared on HotWired, the first commercial web magazine.

The COCONET online service had graphical online banner ads starting in 1988 in San Diego, California.

The PRODIGY service, launched also in 1988, had banner ads as well.

Importance of formats of display ads

Two students of the "Amsterdam school of Communication Research ASCor" have run studies about the audience reactions to different display advertising formats. In particular, they took into consideration two different types of format (sponsored content and banner advertising) to demonstrate that people react and perceive formats in different ways, positive and negative. For this reason, it is important to choose the right format because it will help to make the most of the medium. It is also possible to add:

- Video;
- Rich Media Ads (Expandables): flash files that may expand when the user interacts on mouseover (polite), or auto- initiated (non-polite);
- Overlays: ads that appear above content and that are possible to remove by clicking on a close button;
- Interstitials: Ads that are displayed on web pages before expected content (before the target page is displayed on the user's screen);
- Sponsorship: including a logo or adding a brand to the design of a website. This can also can fall under Native advertising, which is an ad that can seem like Editorial, or "In-Feed", but has really been paid for by the advertiser

To help to better select the right format for the type of ad, Interactive Advertising Bureau has realized a Display Standard Ad Unit Portfolio that works as a guideline that can be followed by the creatives.

- Vertical rectangle: 240 x 400
- Mobile leaderboard: 320 x 50
- Banner: 468 x 60
- Leaderboard: 728 x 90
- Square: 250 x 250
- Small square: 200 x 200
- Large rectangle: 336 x 280
- Inline rectangle: 300 x 250
- Skyscraper: 120 x 600
- Wide skyscraper: 160 x 600
- Half-page: 300 x 600
- Large leaderboard: 970x90
- Large mobile banner: 320 x 100
- Billboard: 970 x 250
- Portrait: 300 x 1050

File:Qxz-ad39.png

Typical web banner, sized 468×60 pixels.

Who works behind display ads

Accounts department

The accounts department meet with the client to define campaign goals and translate those goals into a creative brief to be forwarded to the creative department.

Creative department

The role of the creatives is to give a shape to an ad. They have to find the idea and the most efficient way to push the customer to buy a product or a service. Imagination and innovation are required to develop and to present an advertisement.

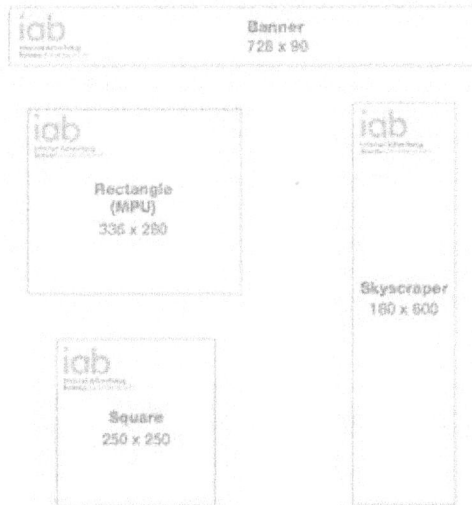

Media planner

People have to test in which way the user experiences all the information of a data visualization. For this reason, they have to study the users' response to sounds, image, and motion. They have to be aware of everything that is digitally consumed, to know all the newest technologies and media solutions, and to help all the other departments to find the best way to reach the object's campaign.

Tools that a media planner uses to buy display advertising include the Google Adwords Display Planner, Quantcast, ComScore, SimilarWeb, Thalamus, Compete, MOAT, and competitive intelligence tools like Adbeat and WhatRunsWhere.

Ad server

The ad server helps manage display advertisements. It is an advertising technology (ad tech) tool that, throughout a platform, administrates the ads and their distribution. It is basically a service or technology for a company that takes care of all the ad campaign programs and by receiving the ad files it is able to allocate them in different websites. The ad server is responsible for things such as the dates by which the campaign has to run on a website; the rapidity in which an ad as to be spread and where (geographic location targeting, language targeting..); controlling that an ad is not overseen by a user by limiting the number of visualisations; proposing an ad on past behaviour targeting.

There are different types of ad servers. There is an ad server for publishers that helps them to launch a new ad on a website by listing the highest ads' price on its and to follow the ad's growth by registering how many users it has reached. There is an ad server for advertisers that helps them by sending the ads in the form of HTML codes to each publisher. In this way, it is possible to open the ad in every moment and make changes of frequency for example, at all times. Lastly, there is an ad server for ad networks that provides information as in which network the publisher is registering an income and which is the daily revenue.

Programmatic Display Advertising

Programmatic or Real Time Bidding (RTB) has revolutionised the way display advertising is bought and managed in recent years. Rather than placing a booking for advertising directly with a website, advertisers will manage their activity through a technology platform (Demand Side Platform) and bid to advertise to people in real time across multiple websites based on targeting criteria.

This method of advertising has fast grown in popularity as it allows for more control for the advertiser (or agency) and means they can control the person that they advertise to rather than just the website. It has become a threat to website operators and generally the cost paid for advertising in this way is less than the old method and so the earning potential for them is reduced.

Programmatic is not without its drawbacks however as without the appropriate management adverts can appear against unsavoury content or inappropriate news topics. This issue became front page news in Feb 2017 when advertisers on Youtube were found to be showing on terror group websites and fake news sites. As a result a number of major advertisers paused all of their online advertising until they could put the appropriate measures in place to prevent this occurring again.

Email marketing

Part of a series on
Internet marketing
• Search engine optimization
• Local search engine optimisation
• Social media marketing
• Email marketing
• Referral marketing
• Content marketing
• Native advertising
Search engine marketing
• Pay-per-click
• Cost per impression
• Search analytics
• Web analytics
Display advertising
• Ad blocking
• Contextual advertising
• Behavioral targeting
Affiliate marketing
• Cost per action
• Revenue sharing
Mobile advertising
• v
• t
• e^{56}

Email marketing is the act of sending a commercial message, typically to a group of people, using email. In its broadest sense, every email sent to a potential or current customer could be considered email marketing. It usually involves using email to send advertisements, request business, or solicit sales or donations, and is meant to build loyalty, trust, or brand awareness. Marketing emails can be sent to a purchased lead list or a current customer database. The term usually refers to sending email messages with the purpose of enhancing a merchant's relationship with current or previous customers, encouraging customer loyalty and repeat business, acquiring new customers or convincing current customers to purchase something immediately, and sharing third-party ads.

History

Email marketing has evolved rapidly alongside the technological growth of the 21st century. Prior to this growth, when emails were novelties to the majority of customers, email marketing was not as effective. In 1978, Gary Thuerk of Digital Equipment Corporation (DEC) sent out the first mass email to approximately 400 potential clients via the Advanced Research Projects Agency Network (ARPANET). This email resulted in $13 million worth of sales in DEC products, and highlighted the potential of marketing through mass emails. However, as email marketing developed as an effective means of direct communication, users began blocking out content from emails with filters and blocking programs. In order to effectively communicate a message through email, marketers had to develop a way of pushing content through to the end user, without being cut out by automatic filters and spam removing software. This resulted in the birth of triggered marketing emails, which are sent to specific users based on their tracked online browsing patterns.

Historically, it has been difficult to measure the effectiveness of marketing campaigns because target markets cannot be adequately defined. Email marketing carries the benefit of allowing marketers to identify returns on investment and measure and improve efficiency.Wikipedia:Citation needed Email marketing allows marketers to see feedback from users in real time, and to monitor how effective their campaign is in achieving market penetration, revealing a communication channel's scope. At the same time, however, it also means that the more personal nature of certain advertising methods, such as television advertisements, cannot be captured.

Types

Email marketing can be carried out through different types of emails:

Transactional emails

Transactional emails are usually triggered based on a customer's action with a company. To be qualified as transactional or relationship messages, these communications' primary purpose must be "to facilitate, complete, or confirm a commercial transaction that the recipient has previously agreed to enter into with the sender" along with a few other narrow definitions of transactional messaging. Triggered transactional messages include dropped basket messages, password reset emails, purchase or order confirmation emails, order status emails, reorder emails, and email receipts.

The primary purpose of a transactional email is to convey information regarding the action that triggered it. But, due to their high open rates (51.3% compared to 36.6% for email newsletters), transactional emails are an opportunity to introduce or extend the email relationship with customers or subscribers; to anticipate and answer questions; or to cross-sell or up-sell products or services.

Many email newsletter software vendors offer transactional email support, which gives companies the ability to include promotional messages within the body of transactional emails. There are also software vendors that offer specialized transactional email marketing services, which include providing targeted and personalized transactional email messages and running specific marketing campaigns (such as customer referral programs). Wikipedia:Citation needed

Direct emails

Direct email involves sending an email solely to communicate a promotional message (for example, a special offer or a product catalog). Companies usually collect a list of customer or prospect email addresses to send direct promotional messages to, or they rent a list of email addresses from service companies. Safe mail marketing is also used. Wikipedia:Citation needed

Mobile email marketing

Email marketing develops large amountsWikipedia:Vagueness of traffic through smartphones and tablets. Marketers are researching ways to advertise to more users and to make them view advertising for longer. However, the rate of delivery is still relatively low due to better filtering-out of advertising and users having multiple email accounts for different purposes. Because emails are generated according to the tracked behavior of consumers, it is possible to send advertising which is based on the recipient's behavior. Because of this, modern email marketing is perceived more often as a pull strategy rather than a push strategy.Wikipedia:Citation needed

Comparison to traditional mail

There are both advantages and disadvantages to using email marketing in comparison to traditional advertising mail.

Advantages

Email marketing is popular with companies for several reasons:

- An exact return on investment can be tracked ("track to basket") and has proven to be highWikipedia:Vagueness when done properly. Email marketing is often reported as second only to search marketing as the most effective online marketing tactic.
- Email marketing is significantly cheaper and faster than traditional mail, mainly because of the high cost and time required in a traditional mail campaign for producing the artwork, printing, addressing, and mailing.
- Businesses and organizations who send a high volume of emails can use an ESP (email service provider) to gather information about the behavior of the recipients. The insights provided by consumer response to email marketing help businesses and organizations understand and make use of consumer behavior.
- Email provides a cost-effective method to test different marketing content, including visual, creative, marketing copy, and multimedia assets. The data gathered by testing in the email channel can then be used across all channels of marketing campaigns, both print and digital.
- Advertisers can reach substantial numbers of email subscribers who have opted in (i.e., consented) to receive the email.Wikipedia:Citation needed
- Almost half of American Internet users check or send email on a typical day,[57] with emails delivered between 1 am and 5 am local time outperforming those sent at other times in open and click rates.[58,59]
- Email is popular with digital marketers, rising an estimated 15% in 2009 to £292 million in the UK.[60]
- If compared to standard email, direct email marketing produces higher response rate and higher average order value for e-commerce businesses.[61]

Disadvantages

As of mid-2016 email deliverability is still an issue for legitimate marketers. According to the report, legitimate email servers averaged a delivery rate of 73% in the U.S.; six percent were filtered as spam, and 22% were missing. This lags behind other countries: Australia delivers at 90%, Canada at 89%, Britain at 88%, France at 84%, Germany at 80% and Brazil at 79%.[62]

Additionally, consumers receive on average circa 90 emails per day.

Companies considering the use of an email marketing program must make sure that their program does not violate spam laws such as the United States' Controlling the Assault of Non-Solicited Pornography and Marketing Act (CAN-SPAM), the European Privacy and Electronic Communications Regulations 2003, or their Internet service provider's acceptable use policy.

Opt-in email advertising

Opt-in email advertising, or permission marketing, is a method of advertising via email whereby the recipient of the advertisement has consented to receive it. This method is one of several developed by marketers to eliminate the disadvantages of email marketing.[63]

Opt-in email marketing may evolve into a technology that uses a handshake protocol between the sender and receiver. This system is intended to eventually result in a high degree of satisfaction between consumers and marketers. If opt-in email advertising is used, the material that is emailed to consumers will be "anticipated". It is assumed that the recipient wants to receive it, which makes it unlike unsolicited advertisements sent to the consumer. Ideally, opt-in email advertisements will be more personal and relevant to the consumer than untargeted advertisements.Wikipedia:Citation needed

A common example of permission marketing is a newsletter sent to an advertising firm's customers. Such newsletters inform customers of upcoming events or promotions, or new products. In this type of advertising, a company that wants to send a newsletter to their customers may ask them at the point of purchase if they would like to receive the newsletter.

With a foundation of opted-in contact information stored in their database, marketers can send out promotional materials automatically using autoresponders—known as drip marketing. They can also segment their promotions to specific market segments.[64]

Legal requirements

Australia

The Australian Spam Act 2003 is enforced by the Australian Communications and Media Authority, widely known as "ACMA". The act defines the term *unsolicited electronic messages*, states how unsubscribe functions must work for commercial messages, and gives other key information. Fines range with 3 fines of AU$110,000 being issued to Virgin Blue Airlines (2011), Tiger Airways Holdings Limited (2012) and Cellar master Wines Pty Limited (2013).

Canada

The "Canada Anti-Spam Law" (CASL) went into effect on July 1, 2014. CASL requires an explicit or implicit opt-in from users, and the maximum fines for noncompliance are CA$1 million for individuals and $10 million for businesses.

European Union

In 2002 the European Union (EU) introduced the Directive on Privacy and Electronic Communications. Article 13 of the Directive prohibits the use of personal email addresses for marketing purposes. The Directive establishes the opt-in regime, where unsolicited emails may be sent only with prior agreement of the recipient; this does not apply to business email addresses.

The directive has since been incorporated into the laws of member states. In the UK it is covered under the Privacy and Electronic Communications (EC Directive) Regulations 2003[65] and applies to all organizations that send out marketing by some form of electronic communication.

United States

The CAN-SPAM Act of 2003 was passed by Congress as a direct response of the growing number of complaints over spam e-mails.Wikipedia:Citation needed Congress determined that the US government was showing an increased interest in the regulation of commercial electronic mail nationally, that those who send commercial e-mails should not mislead recipients over the source or content of them, and that all recipients of such emails have a right to decline them. The act authorizes a US $16,000 penalty per violation for spamming each individual recipient. However, it does not ban spam emailing outright, but imposes laws on using deceptive marketing methods through headings which are "materially false or misleading". In addition there are conditions which email marketers must meet in terms of their format, their content and labeling. As a result, many commercial email marketers within the United States utilize a service or special software to ensure compliance with the act. A variety of older systems exist that do not ensure compliance with the act. To comply with the act's regulation of commercial email, services also typically require users to authenticate their return address and include a valid physical address, provide a one-click unsubscribe feature, and prohibit importing lists of purchased addresses that may not have given valid permission.Wikipedia:Citation needed

In addition to satisfying legal requirements, email service providers (ESPs) began to help customers establish and manage their own email marketing campaigns. The service providers supply email templates and general best practices, as well as methods for handling subscriptions and cancellations automatically. Some ESPs will provide insight and assistance with deliverability issues for major email providers. They also provide statistics pertaining to the number of messages received and opened, and whether the recipients clicked on any links within the messages.

The CAN-SPAM Act was updated with some new regulations including a no-fee provision for opting out, further definition of "sender", post office or private mail boxes count as a "valid physical postal address" and definition of "person". These new provisions went into effect on July 7, 2008.

Search engine marketing

<indicator name="pp-default"> 🔒 </indicator>

Part of a series on
Internet marketing
• Search engine optimization • Local search engine optimisation • Social media marketing • Email marketing • Referral marketing • Content marketing • Native advertising
Search engine marketing
• Pay-per-click • Cost per impression • Search analytics • Web analytics
Display advertising
• Ad blocking • Contextual advertising • Behavioral targeting
Affiliate marketing
• Cost per action • Revenue sharing
Mobile advertising
• v • t • e[66]

Search engine marketing (**SEM**) is a form of Internet marketing that involves the promotion of websites by increasing their visibility in search engine results pages (SERPs) primarily through paid advertising. SEM may incorporate search engine optimization (SEO), which adjusts or rewrites website content and site architecture to achieve a higher ranking in search engine results pages to enhance pay per click (PPC) listings.

Market

In 2007, U.S. advertisers spent US \$24.6 billion on search engine marketing.[67] In Q2 2015, Google (73.7%) and the Yahoo/Bing (26.3%) partnership accounted for almost 100% of U.S. search engine spend. As of 2006, SEM was growing much faster than traditional advertising and even other channels of online marketing. Managing search campaigns is either done directly with the SEM vendor or through an SEM tool provider. It may also be self-serve or through an advertising agency. As of October 2016, Google leads the global search engine market with a market share of 89.3%. Bing comes second with a market share of 4.36%, Yahoo comes third with a market share of 3.3%, and Chinese search engine Baidu is fourth globally with a share of about 0.68%.

History

As the number of sites on the Web increased in the mid-to-late 1990s, search engines started appearing to help people find information quickly. Search engines developed business models to finance their services, such as pay per click programs offered by Open Text in 1996 and then Goto.com in 1998. Goto.com later changed its name to Overture in 2001, was purchased by Yahoo! in 2003, and now offers paid search opportunities for advertisers through Yahoo! Search Marketing. Google also began to offer advertisements on search results pages in 2000 through the Google AdWords program. By 2007, pay-per-click programs proved to be primary moneymakers for search engines. In a market dominated by Google, in 2009 Yahoo! and Microsoft announced the intention to forge an alliance. The Yahoo! & Microsoft Search Alliance eventually received approval from regulators in the US and Europe in February 2010.

Search engine optimization consultants expanded their offerings to help businesses learn about and use the advertising opportunities offered by search engines, and new agencies focusing primarily upon marketing and advertising through search engines emerged. The term "search engine marketing" was popularized by Danny Sullivan in 2001 to cover the spectrum of activities involved in performing SEO, managing paid listings at the search engines, submitting sites to directories, and developing online marketing strategies for businesses, organizations, and individuals.

Methods and metrics

Search engine marketing uses at least five methods and metrics to optimize websites.Wikipedia:Citation needed

1. Keyword research and analysis involves three "steps": ensuring the site can be indexed in the search engines, finding the most relevant and popular keywords for the site and its products, and using those keywords on the site in a way that will generate and convert traffic. A follow-on effect of keyword analysis and research is the search perception impact. Search perception impact describes the identified impact of a brand's search results on consumer perception, including title and meta tags, site indexing, and keyword focus. As online searching is often the first step for potential consumers/customers, the search perception impact shapes the brand impression for each individual.

2. Website saturation and popularity, or how much presence a website has on search engines, can be analyzed through the number of pages of the site that are indexed by search engines (saturation) and how many backlinks the site has (popularity). It requires pages to contain keywords people are looking for and ensure that they rank high enough in search engine rankings. Most search engines include some form of link popularity in their ranking algorithms. The following are major tools measuring various aspects of saturation and link popularity: Link Popularity, Top 10 Google Analysis, and Marketleap's Link Popularity and Search Engine Saturation.

3. Back end tools, including Web analytic tools and HTML validators, provide data on a website and its visitors and allow the success of a website to be measured. They range from simple traffic counters to tools that work with log files and to more sophisticated tools that are based on page tagging (putting JavaScript or an image on a page to track actions). These tools can deliver conversion-related information. There are three major tools used by EBSCO: (a) log file analyzing tool: WebTrends by NetIQ; (b) tag-based analytic tool: WebSideStory's Hitbox; and (c) transaction-based tool: TeaLeaf RealiTea. Validators check the invisible parts of websites, highlighting potential problems and many usability issues and ensuring websites meet W3C code standards. Try to use more than one HTML validator or spider simulator because each one tests, highlights, and reports on slightly different aspects of your website.

4. Whois tools reveal the owners of various websites and can provide valuable information relating to copyright and trademark issues.

5. Google Mobile-Friendly Website Checker: This test will analyze a URL and report if the page has a mobile-friendly design.[68]

Search engine marketing is a way to create and edit a website which can be relative to the search engines than other pages. It should be also focused on keyword marketing or pay-per-click advertising (PPC). The technology enables advertisers to bid on specific keywords or phrases and ensures ads appear with the results of search engines.

With the development of this system, the price is growing under the high level of competition. Many advertisers prefer to expand their activities, including increasing search engines and adding more keywords. The more advertisers are willing to pay for clicks, the higher the ranking for advertising, which leads to higher traffic.[69] PPC comes at a cost. The higher position is likely to cost $5 for a given keyword, and $4.50 for a third location. A third advertiser earns 10% less than the top advertiser, while reducing traffic by 50%.[70] The investors must consider their return on investment and then determine whether the increase in traffic is worth the increase.

There are many reasons explaining why advertisers choose the SEM strategy. First, creating a SEM account is easy and can build traffic quickly based on the degree of competition. The shopper who USES the search engine to find information tends to trust and focus on the links showed in the results pages. However, a large number of online sellers do not buy search engine optimization to obtain higher ranking lists of search results, but prefer paid links. A growing number of online publishers are allowing search engines such as Google to crawl content on their pages and place relevant ads on it.[71] From an online seller's point of view, this is an extension of the payment settlement and an additional incentive to invest in paid advertising projects. Advertisers with limited advertising budgets are virtually impossible to maintain the highest rankings in the increasingly competitive search market. Therefore, it is difficult to break into the market without a big advertising budget for the top search terms. Google's search engine marketing is one of the western world marketing leader while its search engine marketing is biggest source of profit.[72] Their search engine providers are clearly ahead of yahoo! and Microsoft. The display of unknown search results is free, while advertisers are willing to pay for each click of the ad in the sponsored search results.

Paid inclusion

Paid inclusion involves a search engine company charging fees for the inclusion of a website in their results pages. Also known as sponsored listings, paid inclusion products are provided by most search engine companies either in the main results area or as a separately identified advertising area.

The fee structure is both a filter against superfluous submissions and a revenue generator. Typically, the fee covers an annual subscription for one webpage, which will automatically be catalogued on a regular basis. However, some companies are experimenting with non-subscription based fee structures where purchased listings are displayed permanently. A per-click fee may also apply. Each search engine is different. Some sites allow only paid inclusion, although these have had little success. More frequently, many search engines, like Yahoo!, mix paid inclusion (per-page and per-click fee) with results from web crawling. Others, like Google (and as of 2006, Ask.com), do not let webmasters pay to be in their search engine listing (advertisements are shown separately and labeled as such).

Some detractors of paid inclusion allege that it causes searches to return results based more on the economic standing of the interests of a web site, and less on the relevancy of that site to end-users.

Often the line between pay per click advertising and paid inclusion is debatable. Some have lobbied for any paid listings to be labeled as an advertisement, while defenders insist they are not actually ads since the webmasters do not control the content of the listing, its ranking, or even whether it is shown to any users. Another advantage of paid inclusion is that it allows site owners to specify particular schedules for crawling pages. In the general case, one has no control as to when their page will be crawled or added to a search engine index. Paid inclusion proves to be particularly useful for cases where pages are dynamically generated and frequently modified.

Paid inclusion is a search engine marketing method in itself, but also a tool of search engine optimization, since experts and firms can test out different approaches to improving ranking and see the results often within a couple of days, instead of waiting weeks or months. Knowledge gained this way can be used to optimize other web pages, without paying the search engine company.

Comparison with SEO

SEM is the wider discipline that incorporates SEO. SEM includes both paid search results (using tools like Google Adwords or Bing Ads, formerly known as Microsoft adCenter) and organic search results (SEO). SEM uses paid advertising with AdWords or Bing Ads, pay per click (particularly beneficial for local providers as it enables potential consumers to contact a company directly with one click), article submissions, advertising and making sure SEO has been done. A keyword analysis is performed for both SEO and SEM, but not necessarily at the same time. SEM and SEO both need to be monitored and updated frequently to reflect evolving best practices.

In some contexts, the term *SEM* is used exclusively to mean *pay per click advertising*, particularly in the commercial advertising and marketing communities which have a vested interest in this narrow definition. Such usage excludes the wider search marketing community that is engaged in other forms of SEM such as search engine optimization and search retargeting.

Creating the link between SEO and PPC represents an integral part of the SEM concept. Sometimes, especially when separate teams work on SEO and PPC and the efforts are not synced, positive results of aligning their strategies can be lost. The aim of both SEO and PPC is maximizing the visibility in search and thus, their actions to achieve it should be centrally coordinated. Both teams can benefit from setting shared goals and combined metrics, evaluating data together to determine future strategy or discuss which of the tools works better to get the traffic for selected keywords in the national and local search results. Thanks to this, the search visibility can be increased along with optimizing both conversions and costs.

Another part of SEM is social media marketing (SMM). SMM is a type of marketing that involves exploiting social media to influence consumers that one company's products and/or services are valuable. Some of the latest theoretical advances include search engine marketing management (SEMM). SEMM relates to activities including SEO but focuses on return on investment (ROI) management instead of relevant traffic building (as is the case of mainstream SEO). SEMM also integrates organic SEO, trying to achieve top ranking without using paid means to achieve it, and pay per click SEO. For example, some of the attention is placed on the web page layout design and how content and information is displayed to the website visitor. SEO & SEM are two pillars of one marketing job and they both run side by side to produce much better results than focusing on only one pillar.

Ethical questions

Paid search advertising has not been without controversy and the issue of how search engines present advertising on their search result pages has been the target of a series of studies and reports by *Consumer Reports* WebWatch. The Federal Trade Commission (FTC) also issued a letter in 2002 about the importance of disclosure of paid advertising on search engines, in response to a complaint from Commercial Alert, a consumer advocacy group with ties to Ralph Nader.

Another ethical controversy associated with search marketing has been the issue of trademark infringement. The debate as to whether third parties should have the right to bid on their competitors' brand names has been underway for years. In 2009 Google changed their policy, which formerly prohibited these tactics, allowing 3rd parties to bid on branded terms as long as their landing page in fact provides information on the trademarked term. Though the policy has been changed this continues to be a source of heated debate.

On April 24, 2012 many started to see that Google has started to penalize companies that are buying links for the purpose of passing off the rank. The Google Update was called Penguin. Since then, there have been several different Penguin / Panda updates rolled out by Google. SEM has, however, nothing to do with link buying and focuses on organic SEO and PPC management. As of October 20, 2014 Google has released three official revisions of their Penguin Update.

In 2013, the Tenth Circuit Court of Appeals held in *Lens.com, Inc. v. 1-800 Contacts, Inc.* that online contact lens seller Lens.com did not commit trademark infringement when it purchased search advertisements using competitor 1-800 Contacts' federally registered 1800 CONTACTS trademark as a keyword. In August 2016, the Federal Trade Commission filed an administrative complaint against 1-800 Contacts alleging, among other things, that its trademark enforcement practices in the search engine marketing space have unreasonably restrained competition in violation of the FTC Act. 1-800 Contacts has denied all wrongdoing and is scheduled to appear before an FTC administrative law judge in April 2017.[73]

Examples

AdWords is recognized as a web-based advertising utensil since it adopts keywords which can deliver adverts explicitly to web users looking for information in respect to a certain product or service. It is flexible and provides customizable options like Ad Extensions, access to Non-Search sites, leveraging the Display network to help increase the Brand Awareness. This project is highly practical for advertisers as the project hinges on cost per click (CPC) pricing where you can set the maximum cost per day for the campaign, thus the payment of the service only applies if their advert has been clicked on. SEM companies have embarked on AdWords projects as a way to publicize their SEM and SEO services. This promotion has helped their business elaborate, offering added value to consumers who endeavor to employ AdWords for promoting their products and services. One of the most successful approaches to the strategy of this project was to focus on making sure that PPC advertising funds were prudently invested. Moreover, SEM companies have described AdWords as a fine practical tool for increasing a consumer's investment earnings on Internet advertising. The use of conversion tracking and Google Analytics tools was deemed to be practical for presenting to clients the performance of their canvas from click to conversion. AdWords project has enabled SEM companies to train their clients on the utensil and delivers better performance to the canvass. The assistance of AdWord canvass could contribute to the huge success in the growth of web traffic for a number of its consumer's websites, by as much as 250% in only nine months.

Another way search engine marketing is managed is by contextual advertising. Here marketers place ads on other sites or portals that carry information relevant to their products so that the ads jump into the circle of vision of browsers who are seeking information from those sites. A successful SEM plan is the approach to capture the relationships amongst information searchers, businesses, and search engines. Search engines were not important to some industries in the past, but over the past years the use of search engines for accessing information has become vital to increase business opportunities. The use of SEM strategic tools for businesses such as tourism can attract potential consumers to view their products, but it could also pose various challenges. These challenges could be the competition that companies face amongst their industry and other sources of information that could draw the attention of online consumers. To assist the combat of challenges, the main objective for businesses applying SEM is to improve and maintain their ranking as high as possible on SERPs so that they can gain visibility. Therefore, search engines are adjusting and developing algorithms and the shifting criteria by which web pages are ranked sequentially to combat against search engine misuse and spamming, and to supply the most relevant information to searchers. This could enhance the relationship amongst information searchers, businesses, and search engines by understanding the strategies of marketing to attract business.

Social media marketing

<indicator name="pp-default"> 🔒 </indicator> **Social media marketing** is the use of social media platforms and websites to promote a product or service. Although the terms e-marketing and digital marketing are still dominant in academia, social media marketing is becoming more popular for both practitioners and researchers. Most social media platforms have built-in data analytics tools, which enable companies to track the progress, success, and engagement of ad campaigns. Companies address a range of stakeholders through social media marketing, including current and potential customers, current and potential employees, journalists, bloggers, and the general public. On a strategic level, social media marketing includes the management of a marketing campaign, governance, setting the scope (e.g. more active or passive use) and the establishment of a firm's desired social media "culture" and "tone."

To use social media effectively, firms should learn to allow customers and Internet users to post user-generated content (e.g., online comments, product reviews, etc.), also known as "earned media," rather than use marketer-prepared advertising copy.[74] While often associated with companies, as of 2016, a range of not-for-profit organizations and government organizations are engaging in social media marketing.

Platforms

Social networking websites

Social networking websites allow individuals, businesses and other organizations to interact with one another and build relationships and communities online. When companies join these social channels, consumers can interact with them directly.[75] That interaction can be more personal to users than traditional methods of outbound marketing and advertising. Social networking sites act as word of mouth or more precisely, e-word of mouth. The Internet's ability to reach billions across the globe has given online word of mouth a powerful voice and far reach. The ability to rapidly change buying patterns and product or service acquisition and activity to a growing number of consumers is defined as an influence network. Social networking sites and blogs allow followers to "retweet" or "repost" comments made by others about a product being promoted, which occurs quite frequently on some social media sites. By repeating the message, the user's connections are able to see the message, therefore reaching more people. Because the information about the product is being put out there and is getting repeated, more traffic is brought to the product/company.

Social networking websites are based on building virtual communities that allow consumers to express their needs, wants and values, online. Social media marketing then connects these consumers and audiences to businesses that share the same needs, wants, and values. Through social networking sites, companies can keep in touch with individual followers. This personal interaction can instill a feeling of loyalty into followers and potential customers. Also, by choosing whom to follow on these sites, products can reach a very narrow target audience. Social networking sites also include much information about what products and services prospective clients might be interested in. Through the use of new semantic analysis technologies, marketers can detect buying signals, such as content shared by people and questions posted online. An understanding of buying signals can help sales people target relevant prospects and marketers run micro-targeted campaigns.

To integrate social networks into their marketing strategies, companies have to develop a marketing model. In a marketing model (SNeM2S) based on social networks is provided. The model includes the following steps:

* Selection of the potential social networks to use;
* Setting out a financial plan (regarding hiring social media brand managers or consultants);
* Designing or modifying organizational structures to manage the social network in the companies' market (this may involve adding a social media unit to an existing marketing branch or creating a new social media branch);
* Selection of target market(s);
* Selection of the products, services, brand(s) or company messages which will be promoted;
* Performance measures for the social media strategy such as evaluation, data analytics, etc.

In 2014, over 80% of business executives identified social media as an integral part of their business. Business retailers have seen 133% increases in their revenues from social media marketing.[76]

Mobile phones

Just under half the world's population is currently on the Internet. Roughly 75% of those people are on social media and ¾ of those folks have social media accounts on their mobile phones. Mobile phone usage is beneficial for social media marketing because mobile phones have social networking capabilities, allowing individuals immediate web browsing and access to social network ing sites. Mobile phones have grown at a rapid rate, fundamentally altering the path-to-purchase process by allowing consumers to easily obtain pricing and product information in real time and allowing companies to constantly remind and update their followers. Many companies are now putting QR (Quick Response) codes along with products for individuals to access the company website or online services with their smart phones. Retailers use QR codes to facilitate consumer interaction with brands by linking the code to brand websites, promotions, product information, or any other mobile-enabled content. In addition, Real-time bidding use in the mobile advertising industry is high and rising because of its value for on-the-go web browsing. In 2012, Nexage, a provider of real time bidding in mobile advertising, reported a 37% increase in revenue each month. Adfonic, another mobile advertisement publishing platform, reported an increase of 22 billion ad requests that same year.

Mobile devices and The internet also influence the way consumers interact with media and has many further implications for TV ratings, advertising, mobile commerce and more. Mobile media consumption such as mobile audio streaming or mobile video are on the rise – in the United States, more than 100 million users are projected to access online video content via mobile device. Mobile video revenue consists of pay-per-view downloads, advertising, and subscriptions. As of 2013, worldwide mobile phone Internet user penetration was 73.4%. In 2017, figures suggest that more than 90% of Internet users will access online content through their phones.

Strategies

There are two basic strategies for engaging the social media as marketing tools:

Passive approach

Social media can be a useful source of market information and a way to hear customer perspectives. Blogs, content communities, and forums are platforms where individuals share their reviews and recommendations of brands, products, and services. Businesses are able to tap and analyze the customer voices and feedback generated in social media for marketing purposes; in this sense the social media is a relatively inexpensive source of market intelligence which can be used by marketers and managers to track and respond to consumer-identified problems and detect market opportunities. For example, the Internet erupted with videos and pictures of iPhone 6 "bend test" which showed that the coveted phone could be bent by hand pressure. The so-called "bend gate" controversy created confusion amongst customers who had waited months for the launch of the latest rendition of the iPhone. However, Apple promptly issued a statement saying that the problem was extremely rare and that the company had taken several steps to make the mobile device's case stronger and robust. Unlike traditional market research methods such as surveys, focus groups, and data mining which are time-consuming and costly, and which take weeks or even months to analyze, marketers can use social media to obtain 'live' or "real time" information about consumer behavior and viewpoints on a company's brand or products. This can be useful in the highly dynamic, competitive, fast-paced and global marketplace of the 2010s.

Active approach

Social media can be used not only as public relations and direct marketing tools but also as communication channels targeting very specific audiences with social media influencers and social media personalities and as effective customer engagement tools. Technologies predating social media, such as broadcast TV and newspapers can also provide advertisers with a fairly targeted audience, given that an ad placed during a sports game broadcast or in the sports section of a newspaper is likely to be read by sports fans. However, social media websites can target niche markets even more precisely. Using digital tools such as Google Adsense, advertisers can target their ads to very specific demographics, such as people who are interested in social entrepreneurship, political activism associated with a particular political party, or video gaming. Google Adsense does this by looking for keywords in social media user's online posts and comments. It would be hard for a TV station or paper-based newspaper to provide ads that are this targeted (though not impossible, as can be seen with "special issue" sections on niche issues, which newspapers can use to sell targeted ads).

Social networks are, in many cases, a good tool for avoiding costly market research. They are the shortest, fastest and most direct way to reach an audience through a person who, in that specific community, has more credibility than anyone. For example, an athlete 'delivers' to their sponsor a consumer base of millions of people who every day are interested in what they do, what they feel, what they consume. No need to go to a Nikeshop window to see Cristiano Ronaldo's latest boots. He sells them for you directly via a Tweet.

Facebook and LinkedIn are leading social media platforms where users can hyper-target their ads. Hypertargeting not only uses public profile information but also information users submit but hide from others. There are several examples of firms initiating some form of online dialog with the public to foster relations with customers. According to Constantinides, Lorenzo and Gómez Borja (2008) "Business executives like Jonathan Swartz, President and CEO of Sun Microsystems, Steve Jobs CEO of Apple Computers, and McDonalds Vice President Bob Langert post regularly in their CEO blogs, encouraging customers to interact and freely express their feelings, ideas, suggestions, or remarks about their postings, the company or its products". Using customer influencers (for example popular bloggers) can be a very efficient and cost-effective method to launch new products or services[77] Narendra Modi current prime minister of India ranks only second after President Barack Obama in a number of fans on his official Facebook page at 21.8 million and counting.[78] Modi employed social media platforms to circumvent traditional media channels to reach out to the young and urban population of India which is estimated to be 200 million.

Engagement

In the context of the social web, engagement means that customers and stakeholders, such as consumer advocacy groups and groups that criticize companies (e.g., lobby groups or advocacy organizations) are active participants rather than passive viewers. Social media use in a business or political context allows all consumers/citizens to express and share an opinion about a company's products, services or business practices, or a government's actioins. Each participating customer or non-customer (or citizen) who is participating online via social media becomes part of the marketing department (or a challenge to the marketing effort), as other customers read their positive or negative comments or reviews. Getting consumers and potential consumers (or citizens) to be engaged online is fundamental to successful social media marketing. With the advent of social media marketing, it has become increasingly important to gain customer interest in products and services, which can eventually be translated into buying behavior (or voting or donating behavior in a political context). New online marketing concepts of engagement and loyalty have emerged which aim to build customer participation and brand reputation.

Engagement in social media for the purpose of a social media strategy is divided into two parts. The first is proactive, regular posting of new online content (digital photos, digital videos, text) and conversations, as well as the sharing of content and information from others via weblinks. The second part is reactive conversations with social media users responding to those who reach out to your social media profiles through commenting or messaging[79] Traditional media such as TV news shows are limited to one-way interaction with customers or 'push and tell' where only specific information is given to the customer with few or limited mechanisms to obtain customer feedback. Traditional media such as paper newspapers, of course, do give readers the option of sending a letter to the editor, but this is a relatively slow process, as the editorial board has to review the letter and decide if it is appropriate for publication. On the other hand, social media is participative and open, as participants are able to instantly share their views on brands, products, and services. Traditional media gave control of message to the marketer, whereas social media shifts the balance to the consumer (or citizen).

Campaigns

Betty White

Social networking sites can have a large impact on the outcome of events. In 2010, a Facebook campaign surfaced in the form of a petition. Users virtually signed a petition asking NBC Universal to have actress Betty White host *Saturday Night Live*. Once signed, users forwarded the petition to all of their followers. The petition went viral and on May 8, 2010, Betty White hosted *SNL*.

2008 US presidential election

The 2008 US presidential campaign had a huge presence on social networking sites. Barack Obama, a virtually unknown Democratic candidate, utilized 15 different social media websites to form relationships with the millions of American citizens who utilize those networks. His social networking profile pages were constantly being updated and interacting with followers. By the end of his campaign, Obama had 5 million social media network supporters (2.5 million on Facebook and 115,000 on Twitter). The use of social networking sites in his marketing campaign gave Barack Obama's campaign access to e-mail addresses, as posted on social network profile pages. This allowed the Democratic Party to launch e-mail campaigns asking for votes and campaign donations.

Local businesses

Small businesses also use social networking sites as a promotional technique. Businesses can follow individuals social networking site uses in the local area and advertise specials and deals. These can be exclusive and in the form of "get a free drink with a copy of this tweet". This type of message encourages other locals to follow the business on the sites in order to obtain the promotional deal. In the process, the business is getting seen and promoting itself (brand visibility).

Small businesses also use social networking sites to develop their own market research on new products and services. By encouraging their customers to give feedback on new product ideas, businesses can gain valuable insights on whether a product may be accepted by their target market enough to merit full production, or not. In addition, customers will feel the company has engaged them in the process of co-creation—the process in which the business uses customer feedback to create or modify a product or service the filling a need of the target market. Such feedback can present in various forms, such as surveys, contests, polls, etc.

Social networking sites such as LinkedIn, also provide an opportunity for small businesses to find candidates to fill staff positions.[80]

Of course, review sites, such as Yelp, also help small businesses to build their reputation beyond just brand visibility. Positive customer peer reviews help to influence new prospects to purchase goods and services more than company advertising.[81]

As the social media world continues to grow, so does the need to reach customers on social networks. 70% of the U.S. Population has some form of social media profile, and by 2018 that number is projected to be 2.8 Billion.Wikipedia:Citation needed Small businesses can benefit from social media marketing, due to its little to no start up costs which can decrease marketing costs, giving a personality to their brand, increased brand recognition, and higher conversion rates. Engaging customers in the 21st century is now only a click away.Wikipedia:Citation needed

Kony 2012

A short film released on March 5, 2012, by humanitarian group Invisible Children, Inc. This 29-minute video aimed at making Joseph Kony, an International Criminal Court fugitive, famous worldwide in order to have support for his arrest by December 2012—the time when the campaign ends. The video went viral within the first six days after its launch, reaching 100 million views on both YouTube and Vimeo. According to research done by Visible Measures, the Kony 2012 short film became the fastest growing video campaign, and most viral video, to reach 100 million views in 6 days followed by Susan Boyle performance on Britain's Got Talent that reached 70 million views in 6 days.

Nike #MakeItCount

In early 2012, Nike introduced its Make It Count social media campaign. The campaign kickoff began YouTubers Casey Neistat and Max Joseph launching a YouTube video, where they traveled 34,000 miles to visit 16 cities in 13 countries. They promoted the #makeitcount hashtag, which millions of consumers shared via Twitter and Instagram by uploading photos and sending tweets. The #MakeItCount YouTube video went viral and Nike saw an 18% increase in profit in 2012, the year this product was released.

Lay's-Do Us a Flavor

In 2012, Lays created an annual social media campaign that allowed fans to create their own flavor for a $1 million prize for whatever flavor was voted the best. After 3.8 million submissions from fans who participated, the top three choices were Cheesy Garlic Bread, Chicken & Waffles, and Sriracha. The fans were now able to purchase the three flavors in stores then cast their vote on Facebook or Twitter for the best flavor. Lays gained a 12% increase in sales during the contest. Garlic Cheesy Bread was eventually named the winner of the contest.[82]

Purposes and tactics

One of the main purposes of employing social media in marketing is as a communications tool that makes the companies accessible to those interested in their product and makes them visible to those who have no knowledge of their products. These companies use social media to create buzz, and learn from and target customers. It's the only form of marketing that can finger consumers at each and every stage of the consumer decision journey. Marketing through social media has other benefits as well. Of the top 10 factors that correlate with a strong Google organic search, seven are social media dependent. This means that if brands are less or non-active on social media, they tend to show up less on Google searches. While platforms such as Twitter, Facebook, and Google+ have a larger number of monthly users, the visual media sharing based mobile platforms, however, garner a higher interaction rate in comparison and have registered the fastest growth and have changed the ways in which consumers engage with brand content. Instagram has an interaction rate of 1.46% with an average of 130 million users monthly as opposed to Twitter which has a .03% interaction rate with an average of 210 million monthly users. Unlike traditional media that are often cost-prohibitive to many companies, a social media strategy does not require astronomical budgeting.

To this end, companies make use of platforms such as Facebook, Twitter, YouTube, and Instagram to reach audiences much wider than through the use of traditional print/TV/radio advertisements alone at a fraction of the cost, as most social networking sites can be used at little or no cost (however, some websites charge companies for premium services). This has changed the ways that companies approach to interact with customers, as a substantial percentage of consumer interactions are now being carried out over online platforms with much higher visibility. Customers can now post reviews of products and services, rate customer service, and ask questions or voice concerns directly to companies through social media platforms. Thus social media marketing is also used by businesses in order to build relationships of trust with consumers. To this aim, companies may also hire personnel to specifically handle these social media interactions, who usually report under the title of Online community managers. Handling these interactions in a satisfactory manner can result in an increase of consumer trust. To both this aim and to fix the public's perception of a company, 3 steps are taken in order to address consumer concerns, identifying the extent of the social chatter, engaging the influencers to help, and developing a proportional response.

Twitter

Twitter allows companies to promote their products in short messages known as tweets limited to 140 characters which appear on followers' Home timelines. Tweets can contain text, Hashtag, photo, video, Animated GIF, Emoji, or links to the product's website and other social media profiles, etc.[83] Twitter is also used by companies to provide customer service. Some companies make support available 24/7 and answer promptly, thus improving brand loyalty and appreciation.

Facebook

Facebook pages are far more detailed than Twitter accounts. They allow a product to provide videos, photos, and longer descriptions, and testimonials as other followers can comment on the product pages for others to see. Facebook can link back to the product's Twitter page as well as send out event reminders. As of May 2015, 93% of businesses marketers use Facebook to promote their brand. A study from 2011 attributed 84% of "engagement" or clicks to Likes that link back to Facebook advertising. By 2014, Facebook had restricted the content published from businesses' and brands' pages. Adjustments in Facebook algorithms have reduced the audience for non-paying business pages (that have at least 500,000 "Likes") from 16% in 2012 down to 2% in February 2014.

Google+

Google+, in addition to providing pages and some features of Facebook, is also able to integrate with the Google search engine. Other Google products are also integrated, such as Google Adwords and Google Maps. With the development of Google Personalized Search and other location-based search services, Google+ allows for targeted advertising methods, navigation services, and other forms of location-based marketing and promotion. Google+ can also be beneficial for other digital marketing campaigns, as well as social media marketing. Google+ authorship was known to have a significant benefit on a website's search engine optimization, before the relationship was removed by Google. Google+ is one of the fastest growing social media networks and can benefit almost any business.

LinkedIn

LinkedIn, a professional business-related networking site, allows companies to create professional profiles for themselves as well as their business to network and meet others. Through the use of widgets, members can promote their various social networking activities, such as Twitter stream or blog entries of their product pages, onto their LinkedIn profile page. LinkedIn provides its members the opportunity to generate sales leads and business partners. Members can use "Company Pages" similar to Facebook pages to create an area that will allow business owners to promote their products or services and be able to interact with their customers. Due to spread of spam mail sent to job seeker, leading companies prefer to use LinkedIn for employee's recruitment instead using different a job portal. Additionally, companies have voiced a preference for the amount of information that can be gleaned from a LinkedIn profile, versus a limited email.[84]

Whatsapp

WhatsApp was founded by Jan Koum and Brian Acton.WhatsApp joined Facebook in 2014, but continues to operate as a separate app with a laser focus on building a messaging service that works fast and reliably anywhere in the world.WhatsApp started as an alternative to SMS. Whatsapp now supports sending and receiving a variety of media including text, photos, videos, documents, and location, as well as voice calls. Whatsapp messages and calls are secured with end-to-end encryption, meaning that no third party including WhatsApp can read or listen to them. Whatsapp has a customer base of 1 billion people in over 180 countries.[85,86] It is used to send personalised promotional messages to individual customers. It has plenty of advantages over SMS that includes ability to track how Message Broadcast Performs using blue tick option in Whatsapp. It allows sending messages to Do Not Disturb(DND) customers. Whatsapp is also used to send a series of bulk messages to their targeted customers using broadcast option. Companies started using this to a large extent because it is a cost effective promotional option and quick to spread a message. Still, Whatsapp doesn't allow businesses to place ads in their app.

Yelp

Yelp consists of a comprehensive online index of business profiles. Businesses are searchable by location, similar to Yellow Pages. The website is operational in seven different countries, including the United States and Canada. Business account holders are allowed to create, share, and edit business profiles. They may post information such as the business location, contact information, pictures, and service information. The website further allows individuals to write, post reviews about businesses, and rate them on a five-point scale. Messaging and talk features are further made available for general members of the website, serving to guide thoughts and opinions.

Foursquare

Foursquare is a location-based social networking website, where users can check into locations via a Swarm app on their smartphones. Foursquare allows businesses to create a page or create a new/claim an existing venue.

Instagram

In May 2014, Instagram had over 200 million users. The user engagement rate of Instagram was 15 times higher than of Facebook and 25 times higher than that of Twitter. According to Scott Galloway, the founder of L2 and a professor of marketing at New York University's Stern School of Business, latest studies estimate that 93% of prestige brands have an active presence on Instagram and include it in their marketing mix. When it comes to brands and businesses, Instagram's goal is to help companies to reach their respective audiences through captivating imagery in a rich, visual environment. Moreover, Instagram provides a platform where user and company can communicate publicly and directly, making itself an ideal platform for companies to connect with their current and potential customers.

Many brands are now heavily using this mobile app to boost their marketing strategy. Instagram can be used to gain the necessary momentum needed to capture the attention of the market segment that has an interest in the product offering or services. As Instagram is supported by Apple and android system, it can be easily accessed by smartphone users. Moreover, it can be accessed by the Internet as well. Thus, the marketers see it as a potential platform to expand their brands exposure to the public, especially the younger target group. On top of this, marketers do not only use social media for traditional Internet advertising, but they also encourage users to create attention for a certain brand. This generally creates an opportunity for greater brand exposure. Furthermore, marketers are also using the platform to drive social shopping and inspire people to collect and share pictures of their favorite products. Many big names have already jumped on board: Starbucks, MTV, Nike, Marc Jacobs, and Red Bull are a few examples of multinationals that adopted the mobile photo app early. Fashion blogger Danielle Bernstein, who goes by @weworewhat on Instagram, collaborated with *Harper's Bazaar* to do a piece on how brands are using Instagram to market their products, and how bloggers make money from it. Bernstein, who currently has one and a half million followers on Instagram, and whose "outfit of the day" photos on Snapchat get tens of thousands of screenshots, explained that for a lot of her sponsored posts, she must feature the brand in a certain number of posts, and often cannot wear a competitor's product in the same picture. According to *Harper's Bazaar*, industry estimates say that brands are spending more than $1 billion per year on consumer-generated advertising. Founder of Instagram

Kevin Systrom even went to Paris Fashion week, going to couture shows and meeting with designers to learn more about how style bloggers, editors, and designers are currently dominating much of the content on his application. Instagram has proven itself a powerful platform for marketers to reach their customers and prospects through sharing pictures and brief messages. According to a study by Simply Measured, 71% of the world's largest brands are now using Instagram as a marketing channel. For companies, Instagram can be used as a tool to connect and communicate with current and potential customers. The company can present a more personal picture of their brand, and by doing so the company conveys a better and true picture of itself. The idea of Instagram pictures lies on on-the-go, a sense that the event is happening right now, and that adds another layer to the personal and accurate picture of the company. In fact, Thomas Rankin, co-founder and CEO of the program Dash Hudson, stated that when he approves a blogger's Instagram post before it is posted on the behalf of a brand his company represents, his only negative feedback is if it looks too posed. "It's not an editorial photo," he explained, "We're not trying to be a magazine. We're trying to create a moment." Another option Instagram provides the opportunity for companies to reflect a true picture of the brandfrom the perspective of the customers, for instance, using the user-generated contents thought the hashtags encouragement. Other than the filters and hashtags functions, the Instagram's 15-second videos and the recently added ability to send private messages between users have opened new opportunities for brands to connect with customers in a new extent, further promoting effective marketing on Instagram.

YouTube

YouTube is another popular avenue; advertisements are done in a way to suit the target audience. The type of language used in the commercials and the ideas used to promote the product reflect the audience's style and taste. Also, the ads on this platform are usually in sync with the content of the video requested, this is another advantage YouTube brings for advertisers. Certain ads are presented with certain videos since the content is relevant. Promotional opportunities such as sponsoring a video is also possible on YouTube, "for example, a user who searches for a YouTube video on dog training may be presented with a sponsored video from a dog toy company in results along with other videos." YouTube also enable publishers to earn money through its YouTube Partner Program. Companies can pay YouTube for a special "channel" which promotes the companies products or services.

Social bookmarking sites

Websites such as Delicious, Digg, Slashdot, Diigo, Stumbleupon, and Reddit are popular social bookmarking sites used in social media promotion. Each of these sites is dedicated to the collection, curation, and organization of links to other websites that users deem to be of good quality. This process is "crowd-sourced", allowing amateur social media network members to sort and prioritize links by relevance and general category. Due to the large user bases of these websites, any link from one of them to another, the smaller website may in a flash crowd, a sudden surge of interest in the target website. In addition to user-generated promotion, these sites also offer advertisements within individual user communities and categories.[87] Because ads can be placed in designated communities with a very specific target audience and demographic, they have far greater potential for traffic generation than ads selected simply through cookie and browser history.[88] Additionally, some of these websites have also implemented measures to make ads more relevant to users by allowing users to vote on which ones will be shown on pages they frequent.[89] The ability to redirect large volumes of web traffic and target specific, relevant audiences makes social bookmarking sites a valuable asset for social media marketers.

Blogs

Platforms like LinkedIn create an environment for companies and clients to connect online. Companies that recognize the need for information, originality/ and accessibility employ blogs to make their products popular and unique/ and ultimately reach out to consumers who are privy to social media. Studies from 2009 show that consumers view coverage in the media or from bloggers as being more neutral and credible than print advertisements, which are not thought of as free or independent. Blogs allow a product or company to provide longer descriptions of products or services, can include testimonials and can link to and from other social network and blog pages. Blogs can be updated frequently and are promotional techniques for keeping customers, and also for acquiring followers and subscribers who can then be directed to social network pages. Online communities can enable a business to reach the clients of other businesses using the platform. To allow firms to measure their standing in the corporate world, sites enable employees to place evaluations of their companies. Some businesses opt out of integrating social media platforms into their traditional marketing regimen. There are also specific corporate standards that apply when interacting online. To maintain an advantage in a business-consumer relationship, businesses have to be aware of four key assets that consumers maintain: information, involvement, community, and control.

Tumblr

Blogging website Tumblr first launched ad products on May 29, 2012. Rather than relying on simple banner ads, Tumblr requires advertisers to create a Tumblr blog so the content of those blogs can be featured on the site. In one year, four native ad formats were created on web and mobile, and had more than 100 brands advertising on Tumblr with 500 cumulative sponsored posts.

Ad formats

* **Sponsored mobile pPost** – Advertisements (Advertisers' blog posts) will show up on user's Dashboard when the user is on a mobile device such as smartphones and tablets, allowing them to like, reblog, and share the sponsored post.
* **Sponsored web post** – "Largest in-stream ad unit on the web" that catches the users' attention when looking at their Dashboard through their computer or laptop. It also allows the viewers to like, reblog, and share it.
* **Sponsored radar** – Radar picks up exceptional posts from the whole Tumblr community based on their originality and creativity. It is placed on the right side next to the Dashboard, and it typically earns 120 million daily impressions. Sponsored radar allows advertisers to place their posts there to have an opportunity to earn new followers, reblogs, and likes.
* **Sponsored spotlight** – Spotlight is a directory of some of the popular blogs throughout the community and a place where users can find new blogs to follow. Advertisers can choose one category out of fifty categories that they can have their blog listed on there.

These posts can be one or more of the following: images, photo sets, animated GIFs, video, audio, and text posts. For the users to differentiate the promoted posts to the regular users' posts, the promoted posts have a dollar symbol on the corner. On May 6, 2014, Tumblr announced customization and theming on mobile apps for brands to advertise.

Advertising campaigns

* **Disney/Pixar's** *Monsters University*: Created a Tumblr account, MU-Grumblr, saying that the account is maintained by a 'Monstropolis transplant' and 'self-diagnosed coffee addict' who is currently a sophomore at Monsters University. A "student" from Monsters University uploaded memes, animated GIFs, and Instagram-like photos that are related to the sequel movie.

- **Apple's iPhone 5c:** Created a Tumblr page, labeling it "Every color has a story" with the website name: "ISee5c". As soon as you visit the website, the page is covered with different colors representing the iPhone 5c phone colors and case colors. When you click on one of the colored section, a 15-second video plays a song and "showcases the dots featured on the rear of the iPhone 5c official cases and on the iOS 7 dynamic wallpapers...", concluding with words that are related to the video's theme.

Marketing techniques

Social media marketing involves the use of social networks, *consumer's online brand-related activities* (COBRA) and *electronic word of mouth* (eWOM) to successfully advertise online. Social networks such as Facebook and Twitter provide advertisers with information about the likes and dislikes of their consumers. This technique is crucial, as it provides the businesses with a "target audience". With social networks, information relevant to the user's likes is available to businesses; who then advertise accordingly. Activities such as uploading a picture of your "new Converse sneakers to Facebook" is an example of a *COBRA*. Electronic recommendations and appraisals are a convenient manner to have a product promoted via "consumer-to-consumer interactions. An example of *eWOM* would be an online hotel review; the hotel company can have two possible outcomes based on their service. A good service would result in a positive review which gets the hotel free advertising via social media. However, a poor service will result in a negative consumer review which can potentially harm the company's reputation.

Social networking sites such as Facebook, Instagram, Twitter, MySpace etc. have all influenced the buzz of word of mouth marketing. In 1999, Misner said that word-of mouth marketing is, "the world's most effective, yet least understood marketing strategy" (Trusov, Bucklin, & Pauwels, 2009, p. 3). Through the influence of opinion leaders, the increased online "buzz" of "word-of-mouth" marketing that a product, service or companies are experiencing is due to the rise in use of social media and smartphones. Businesses and marketers have noticed that, "a persons behaviour is influenced by many small groups" (Kotler, Burton, Deans, Brown, & Armstrong, 2013, p. 189). These small groups rotate around social networking accounts that are run by influential people (opinion leaders or "thought leaders") who have followers of groups. The types of groups (followers) are called:[90] reference groups (people who know each other either face-to-face or have an indirect influence on a persons attitude or behaviour); membership groups (a person has a direct influence on a person's attitude or behaviour); and aspirational groups (groups which an individual wishes to belong to).

Marketers target influential people on social media who are recognised as being opinion leaders and opinion-formers to send messages to their target audiences and amplify the impact of their message. A social media post by an opinion leader can have a much greater impact (via the forwarding of the post or "liking" of the post) than a social media post by a regular user. Marketers have come to the understanding that "consumers are more prone to believe in other individuals" who they trust (Sepp, Liljander, & Gummerus, 2011). OL's and OF's can also send their own messages about products and services they choose (Fill, Hughes, & De Francesco, 2013, p. 216). The reason the opinion leader or formers have such a strong following base is because their opinion is valued or trusted (Clement, Proppe, & Rott, 2007). They can review products and services for their followings, which can be positive or negative towards the brand. OL's and OF's are people who have a social status and because of their personality, beliefs, values etc. have the potential to influence other people (Kotler, Burton, Deans, Brown, & Armstrong, 2013, p. 189). They usually have a large number of followers otherwise known as their reference, membership or aspirational group (Kotler, Burton, Deans, Brown, & Armstrong, 2013, p. 189. By having an OL or OF support a brands product by posting a photo, video or written recommendation on a blog, the following may be influenced and because they trust the OL/OF a high chance of the brand selling more products or creating a following base. Having an OL/OF helps spread word of mouth talk amongst reference groups and/or memberships groups e.g. family, friends, work-friends etc. (Kotler, Burton, Deans, Brown, & Armstrong, 2013, p. 189).[91,92] The adjusted communication model shows the use of using opinion leaders and opinion formers. The sender/source gives the message to many, many OL's/OF's who pass the message on along with their personal opinion, the receiver (followers/groups) form their own opinion and send their personal message to their group (friends, family etc.) (Dahlen, Lange, & Smith, 2010, p. 39).[93]

The platform of social media is another channel or site that business' and brands must seek to influence the content of. In contrast with pre-Internet marketing, such as TV ads and newspaper ads, in which the marketer controlled all aspects of the ad, with social media, users are free to post comments right below an online ad or an online post by a company about its product. Companies are increasing using their social media strategy as part of their traditional marketing effort using magazines, newspapers, radio advertisements, television advertisements. Since in the 2010s, media consumers are often using multiple platforms at the same time (e.g., surfing the Internet on a tablet while watching a streaming TV show), marketing content needs to be consistent across all platforms, whether traditional or new media. Heath (2006) wrote about the extent of attention businesses should give to their social media sites. It is about finding a balance between frequently posting but not over posting. There is a lot more attention to be paid towards social media sites because people need updates to gain brand recognition. Therefore, a lot more content is need and this can often be unplanned content.

Planned content begins with the creative/marketing team generating their ideas, once they have completed their ideas they send them off for approval. There is two general ways of doing so. The first is where each sector approves the plan one after another, editor, brand, followed by the legal team (Brito, 2013). Sectors may differ depending on the size and philosophy of the business. The second is where each sector is given 24 hours (or such designated time) to sign off or disapprove. If no action is given within the 24-hour period the original plan is implemented. Planned content is often noticeable to customers and is un-original or lacks excitement but is also a safer option to avoid unnecessary backlash from the public.[94] Both routes for planned content are time consuming as in the above; the first way to approval takes 72 hours to be approved. Although the second route can be significantly shorter it also holds more risk particularly in the legal department.

Unplanned content is an 'in the moment' idea, "a spontaneous, tactical reaction." (Cramer, 2014, p. 6). The content could be trending and not have the time to take the planned content route. The unplanned content is posted sporadically and is not calendar/date/time arranged (Deshpande, 2014).[95] Issues with unplanned content revolve around legal issues and whether the message being sent out represents the business/brand accordingly. If a company sends out a Tweet or Facebook message too hurriedly, the company may unintentionally use insensitive language or messaging that could alienate some consumers. For example, celebrity chef Paula Deen was criticized after she made a social media post commenting about HIV-AIDS and South Africa; her message was deemed to be offensive by many observers. The main difference between planned and unplanned is the time to approve the content. Unplanned content must still be approved by marketing managers, but in a much more rapid manner e.g. 1–2 hours or less. Sectors may miss errors because of being hurried. When using unplanned content Brito (2013) says, "be prepared to be reactive and respond to issues when they arise." Brito (2013) writes about having a, "crisis escalation plan", because, "It will happen". The plan involves breaking down the issue into topics and classifying the issue into groups. Colour coding the potential risk "identify and flag potential risks" also helps to organise an issue. The problem can then be handled by the correct team and dissolved more effectively rather than any person at hand trying to solve the situation.

Implications on traditional advertising

Minimizing use

Traditional advertising techniques include print and television advertising. The Internet has already overtaken television as the largest advertising market.[96] Web sites often include the banner or pop-up ads. Social networking sites don't always have ads. In exchange, products have entire pages and are able to interact with users. Television commercials often end with a spokesperson asking viewers to check out the product website for more information. While briefly popular, print ads included QR codes on them. These QR codes can be scanned by cell phones and computers, sending viewers to the product website. Advertising is beginning to move viewers from the traditional outlets to the electronic ones.Wikipedia:Citation needed

While traditional media, like newspapers and television advertising, are largely overshadowed by the rise of social media marketing, there is still a place for traditional marketing. For example, with newspapers, readership over the years has shown a decline. However, readership with newspapers is still fiercely loyal to print-only media. 51% of newspaper readers only read the newspaper in its print form, making well-placed ads valuable.

Leaks

The Internet and social networking leaks are one of the issues facing traditional advertising. Video and print ads are often leaked to the world via the Internet earlier than they are scheduled to premiere. Social networking sites allow those leaks to go viral, and be seen by many users more quickly. The time difference is also a problem facing traditional advertisers. When social events occur and are broadcast on television, there is often a time delay between airings on the east coast and west coast of the United States. Social networking sites have become a hub of comment and interaction concerning the event. This allows individuals watching the event on the west coast (time-delayed) to know the outcome before it airs. The 2011 Grammy Awards highlighted this problem. Viewers on the west coast learned who won different awards based on comments made on social networking sites by individuals watching live on the east coast. Since viewers knew who won already, many tuned out and ratings were lower. All the advertisement and promotion put into the event was lost because viewers didn't have a reason to watch. Wikipedia:Manual_of_Style/Words_to_watch#Unsupported_attributions

Mishaps

Social media marketing provides organizations with a way to connect with their customers. However, organizations must protect their information as well as closely watch comments and concerns on the social media they use. A flash poll done on 1225 IT executives from 33 countries revealed that social media mishaps caused organizations a combined $4.3 million in damages in 2010. The top three social media incidents an organization faced during the previous year included employees sharing too much information in public forums, loss or exposure of confidential information, and increased exposure to litigation. Due to the viral nature of the Internet, a mistake by a single employee has in some cases shown to result in devastating consequences for organizations. An example of a social media mishap includes designer Kenneth Cole's Twitter mishap in 2011. When Kenneth Cole tweeted, "Millions are in uproar in #Cairo. Rumor has they heard our new spring collection is now available online at [Kenneth Cole's website]".[97] This reference to the 2011 Egyptian revolution drew an objection from the public; it was widely objected to on the Internet. Kenneth Cole realized his mistake shortly after and responded with a statement apologizing for the tweet.[98]

In 2012 during Hurricane Sandy, Gap sent out a tweet to its followers telling them to stay safe but encouraged them to shop online and offered free shipping. The tweet was deemed insensitive, and Gap eventually took it down and apologized.[99] Numerous additional online marketing mishap examples exist. Examples include a YouTube video of a Domino's Pizza employee violating health code standards, which went viral on the Internet and later resulted in felony charges against two employees. A Twitter hashtag posted by McDonald's in 2012 attracting attention due to numerous complaints and negative events customers experienced at the chain store; and a 2011 tweet posted by a Chrysler Group employee that no one in Detroit knows how to drive.[100] When the Link REIT opened a Facebook page to recommend old-style restaurants, the page was flooded by furious comments criticizing the REIT for having forced a lot of restaurants and stores to shut down; it had to terminate its campaign early amid further deterioration of its corporate image.[101]

Ethics

The code of ethics that is affiliated with traditional marketing can also be applied to social media. However, with social media being so personal and international, there is another list of complications and challenges that come along with being ethical online. With the invention of social media, the marketer no longer has to focus solely on the basic demographics and psychographics given from television and magazines, but now they can see what consumers like to hear from advertisers, how they engage online, and what their needs

and wants are. The general concept of being ethical while marking on social network sites is to be honest with the intentions of the campaign, avoid
false advertising, be aware of user privacy conditions (which means not using
consumers' private information for gain), respect the dignity of persons in the
shared online community, and claim responsibility for any mistakes or mishaps
that are results of your marketing campaign. Most social network marketers
use websites like Facebook and MySpace to try to drive traffic to another website. While it is ethical to use social networking websites to spread a message to
people who are genuinely interested, many people game the system with auto-
friend adding programs and spam messages and bulletins. Social networking
websites are becoming wise to these practices, however, and are effectively
weeding out and banning offenders.

In addition, social media platforms have become extremely aware of their users
and collect information about their viewers to connect with them in various
ways. Social-networking website Facebook Inc. is quietly working on a new
advertising system that would let marketers target users with ads based on the
massive amounts of information people reveal on the site about themselves.
This may be an unethical or ethical feature to some individuals. Some people
may react negatively because they believe it is an invasion of privacy. On the
other hand, some individuals may enjoy this feature because their social network recognizes their interests and sends them particular advertisements pertaining to those interests. Consumers like to network with people who have
interests and desires that are similar to their own. Individuals who agree to
have their social media profile public, should be aware that advertisers have
the ability to take information that interests them to be able to send them information and advertisements to boost their sales. Managers invest in social
media to foster relationships and interact with customers. This is an ethical
way for managers to send messages about their advertisements and products
to their consumers.

Since social media marketing first came to be, strategists and markets have
been getting smarter and more careful with the way they go about collecting
information and distributing advertisements. With the presence of data collecting companies, there is no longer a need to target specific audiences. This can
be seen as a large ethical gray area. For many users, this is a breach of privacy,
but there are no laws that prevent these companies from using the information
provided on their websites. Companies like Equifax, Inc., TransUnion Corp,
and LexisNexis Group thrive on collecting and sharing personal information
of social media users. In 2012, Facebook purchased information from 70 million households from a third party company called Datalogix. Facebook later
revealed that they purchased the information in order to create a more efficient
advertising service.

Facebook had an estimated 144.27 million views in 2016, approximately 12.9 million per month. Despite this high volume of traffic, very little has been done to protect the millions of users who log on to Facebook and other social media platforms each month. President Barack Obama tried to work with the Federal Trade Commission (FTC) to attempt to regulate data mining. He proposed the Privacy Bill of Rights, which would protect the average user from having their private information downloaded and shared with third party companies. The proposed laws would give the consumer more control over what information companies can collect. President Obama was unable to pass most of these laws through congress, and it is unsure what President Trump will do with regards to social media marketing ethics.

Metrics

Web site reports

This involves tracking the volume of visits, leads, and customers to a website from the individual social channel. Google Analytics is a free tool that shows the behavior and other information, such as demographics and device type used, of website visitors from social networks. This and other commercial offers can aid marketers in choosing the most effective social networks and social media marketing activities.

Return on investment data

The end goal of any marketing effort is to generate sales. Although social media is a useful marketing tool, it is often difficult to quantify to what extent it is contributing to profit. ROI can be measured by comparing marketing analytic value to contact database or CRM and connect marketing efforts directly to sales activity.

Customer response rates

Several customers are turning towards social media to express their appreciation or frustration with brands, product or services. Therefore, marketers can measure the frequency of which customers are discussing their brand and judge how effective their SMM strategies are. In recent studies, 72% of people surveyed expressed that they expected a response to their complaints on Twitter within an hour.

Reach and virality

Popular social media such as Facebook, Twitter, LinkedIn, and other social networks can provide marketers with a hard number of how large their audience is nevertheless a large audience may not always translate into a large sales volumes. Therefore, an effective SMM cannot be measured by a large audience but rather by vigorous audience activity such as social shares, re-tweets etc.

External links

Library resources about **social media marketing**
• Online books[102] • Resources in your library[103] • Resources in other libraries[104]

• Kang, Juhee (2015). *Social media marketing*[105] (dissertation). Journal of Marketing. Retrieved 8 February 2015.

Video advertising

The term **video advertising** encompasses online display advertisements that have video within them, but it is generally accepted that it refers to advertising that occurs before, during and/or after a video stream on the internet.

The advertising units used in this instance are pre-roll, mid-roll, and post-roll and all of these ad units are like the traditional spot advertising you see on television, although often they are "cut-down" to be a shorter version than their TV counterparts if they are run online.

Broadcast websites such as Sky.com and itv.com have such advertising on their sites, as do newspaper websites such as *The Telegraph*, and *The Guardian*. In 2010, video ads accounted for 12.8% of all videos viewed and 1.2% of all minutes spent viewing video online.[106]

In July 2014 Facebook paid an estimated $400 million to acquire LiveRail, a video advertising distributor which uses Real-time bidding to place more than 7 billion video ads a month.

Video ad formats

According to Interactive Advertising Bureau (IAB) guidelines, there are three types of video ad formats:[107]

- Linear video ads - the ads are presented before, in the middle of, or after the video content is consumed by the user, in very much the same way a TV commercial can play before, during or after the chosen program.
- Non-linear video ads - the ads run concurrently with the video content so the users see the ad while viewing the content.
- Companion ads - commonly text, display ads, rich media, or skins that wrap around the video experience.

Digital Marketing Strategy

Digital marketing system

A **digital marketing system** (**DMS**) is a method of centralized channel distribution used primarily by SaaS products. It combines a content management system (CMS) with syndication across web, mobile, scannable surface, and social channels.

Web

A DMS publishes to web channels, usually in the form of a stand-alone website. It can manage any part of the web process, including web design, web hosting, domain registering, marketing, content creation and other standard methods of web promotion. The goal of web publication is to give the user a digital 'home' on the web, where clients, guests, fans and other web browsers arrive as a destination. Other methods of digital marketing often work to drive traffic to the web channel.

An example of a SaaS DMS services is HubSpot.

Social

A DMS publishes to popular social channels, including Facebook and Twitter as a means to communicate with fans, friends, followers and customers and drive traffic to the user's website. Social publication can take the form of a status update, a text message, a 'tweet', a photo, a video and many other means of social communication. The idea is to find browsers in social spaces who might not otherwise be targeted. And that of which helps to communicate including social media networks for example Facebook and Twitter.

Mobile

A DMS publishes to mobile devices, offering unique content formatted for those devices, such as the iPhone, iPad and Android phones. Mobile publication often takes the form of a mobile optimized website theme, with larger navigation and a cleaner user interface. Mobile publication can also include 'apps' for devices that support them, 'push' notifications and SMS texting marketing.

Gaming is also a new form of Digital marketing, where creators custom make games fit for a certain brand. It is used with a larger navigations and an interface. It is the key factor to where mobile publication is included within the services.

Scannable surface

A set of scannable surface includes tablet PC, publishing material, TV etc media. QR code enables traditional marketing channels to be utilized for new digital transform. A quick scan on the QR code can guide viewers directly to the information they need without spending time on browsing and searching, and the most valuable method of using QR code scan is to link to purchase basket.

NFC or Near field communication is a growing technology used in information sharing, that is, cash transactions, access inform and other personal information.

Appendix

References

[1] How To Embrace The Five Steps Of Data-Driven Marketing https://www.forbes.com/sites/lisaarthur/2013/10/17/how-to-embrace-the-five-steps-of-data-driven-marketing/#6111d8f140b9 Published by Forbes, October 17, 2013; accessed 17 January, 2017

[2] http://eds.a.ebscohost.com/eds/pdfviewer/pdfviewer?sid=bdb6c9a5-c01c-4b99-8b9d-611e4500abf0%2540sessionmgr4003&vid=1&hid=4202

[3] Sakas, D. P., Dimitrios, N. K., & Kavoura, A. (2015). The Development of Facebook's Competitive Advantage for Brand Awareness. Procedia Economics And Finance, 24(International Conference on Applied Economics (ICOAE) 2015, 2–4 July 2015, Kazan, Russia), 589-597.

[4] Öztürk, C. M. (Ed.) (2013) Dijital İletişim ve Yeni Medya, Anadolu Üniversitesi Yayını: 2956, Eskişehir.

[5] Hudson, S., Huang, L., Roth, M. S., & Madden, T. J. (2016). The influence of social media interactions on consumer–brand relationships: A three-country study of brand perceptions and marketing behaviors. *International Journal Of Research In Marketing*, 3327-41.

[6] PricewaterhouseCoopers (2013), "2012 Internet Advertising Revenue Full-Year Report," April, AdvertisingRevenueReportFY2012POSTED.pdf/

[7] Chatterjee, Patrali (2001), "Beyond CPMs and Clickthroughs: Understanding Consumer Interaction with Web Advertising," in Internet Marketing Research: Theory and Practice, Ook Lee, ed., Hershey, PA: Idea Group, 209–16.

[8] Fill, C. (2006). Marketing communications. 1st ed. Harlow: FT Prentice Hall, pp.372-373.

[9] Parmenter, D. (2007). Key performance indicators. 1st ed. Hoboken, N.J.: John Wiley & Sons.

[10] Marr, B. (2012). Key performance indicators. 1st ed. Harlow, England ; ; New York: Pearson Financial Times Pub.

[11] French, A. and Smith, G. (2013). Measuring brand association strength: a consumer based brand equity approach. European Journal of Marketing, 47(8), pp.1356-1367.

[12] McCarthy, E.J. (1964), Basic Marketing, Richard D. Irwin, Homewood, IL.

[13] Mercer, D. (1999). Marketing. 1st ed. Oxford [u.a.]: Blackwell.

[14] Booms, B.H. and Bitner, M.J., 1981. Marketing strategies and organization structures for service firms. Marketing of services, 25(3), pp.47-52

[15] Chaffey, D. and Ellis-Chadwick, F. (2012). Digital Marketing: Strategy, Implementation and Practice. 1st ed. Harlow: Pearson Education.

[16] Ryan, D. (2014). Understanding Digital Marketing: Marketing Strategies for Engaging the Digital Generation Ed. 3. 1st ed. Kogan Page.

[17] //en.wikipedia.org/w/index.php?title=Template:Internet_marketing&action=edit

[18] Prussakov, Evgenii (2007). "A Practical Guide to Affiliate Marketing" (pp.16-17), 2007.

[19] Chicago Tribune, October 4, 1995

[20] The Sunsentinal, 1991

[21] PC Week Article, January 9, 1995

[22] Business Wire, January 24, 2000

[23] Business Wire, March 31, 1999

[24] Collins, Shawn (2000-11-10). History of Affiliate Marketing. *ClickZ Network*, 10 November 2000. Retrieved on 2007-10-15 from http://www.clickz.com/showPage.html?page=832131.

[25] Olim, Jason; Olim, Matthew; and Kent, Peter (1999-01). "The CDNOW Story: Rags to Riches on the Internet", *Top Floor Publishing*, January 1999.

[26] Frank Fiore and Shawn Collins, "Successful Affiliate Marketing for Merchants", from pages 12, 13 and 14. *QUE Publishing*, April 2001

[27] Gray, Daniel (1999-11-30). "The Complete Guide to Associate and Affiliate Programs on the Net". *McGraw-Hill Trade*, 30 November 1999.

[28] October 2006, Affiliate Marketing Networks Buyer's Guide (2006) http://www.e-consultancy.com/publications/affiliate-marketing-networks-buyers-guide/, Page 6, *e-Consultancy.com*, retrieved June 25, 2007

[29] Anne Holland, publisher (January 11, 2006), Affiliate Summit 2006 Wrap-Up Report – Commissions to Reach $6.5 Billion in 2006 http://www.marketingsherpa.com/barrier.cfm? contentID=3157, *MarketingSherpa*, retrieved on May 17, 2007

[30] CellarStone Inc. (2006), Sales Commission http://www.qcommission.com/salescommission_details.htm, *QCommission.com*, retrieved June 25, 2007

[31] Tom Taulli (9 November 2005), Creating A Virtual Sales Force https://web.archive.org/web/20100601034247/http://www.forbes.com/2005/11/08/marketing-ecommerce-internet-cx_tt_1109straightup.html, *Forbes.com Business*. Retrieved 14 May 2007.

[32] Danny Sullivan (June 27, 2006), The Daily SearchCast News from June 27, 2006 http://www.webmasterradio.fm/episodes/index.php?showId=30, *WebmasterRadio.fm*, retrieved May 17, 2007

[33] Wayne Porter (September 6, 2006), NEW FIRST: LinkShare- Lands' End Versus The Affiliate on Typosquatting http://www.revenews.com/wayneporter/archives/002263.html , *ReveNews*, retrieved on May 17, 2007

[34] Jennifer D. Meacham (July/August 2006), Going Out Is In http://www.revenuetoday.com/story/Going+Out+Is+In, *Revenue Magazine*, published by Montgomery Research Inc, Issue 12., Page 36

[35] http//dispenser.info.tm

[36] Marios Alexandrou (February 4th, 2007), CPM vs. CPC vs. CPA http://www.allthingssem.com/cpm-cpc-cpa/ , *All Things SEM*, retrieved November 11, 2007

[37] Ryan Singel (October 2, 2005), Shady Web of Affiliate Marketing https://www.wired.com/politics/security/news/2005/02/66556, *Wired.com*, retrieved May 17, 2007

[38] Jim Hedger (September 6, 2006), Being a Bigdaddy Jagger Meister http://www.webpronews.com/expertarticles/2006/06/09/being-a-bigdaddy-jagger-meister , *WebProNews.com*, retrieved on December 16, 2007

[39] Spam Recognition Guide for Raters http://www.searchbistro.com/spamguide.doc (Word document) supposedly leaked out from Google http://www.threadwatch.org/node/2709 in 2005. The authenticity of the document was neither acknowledged nor challenged by Google.

[40] December 10, 2002, Online Marketing Service Providers Announce Web Publisher Code of Conduct http://www.cj.com/news/press_releases0102/press_021210.html (contains original CoC text), *CJ.com*, retrieved June 26, 2007

[41] December 12, 2002, LinkShare's Anti-Predatory Advertising Addendum http://www.linkshare.com/press/addendum.html, *LinkShare.com*, retrieved June 26, 2007

[42] ShareASale Affiliate Service Agreement http://www.shareasale.com/agreement.cfm, *ShareASale.com*, retrieved June 26, 2007

[43] April 20, 2007, AdWare Class Action Lawsuit against - ValueClick, Commission Junction and beFree http://www.cjclassaction.com/, *Law Firms of Nassiri & Jung LLP and Hagens Berman*, retrieved from CJClassAction.com on June 26, 2007

[44] FTC Publishes Final Guides Governing Endorsements, Testimonials http://www.ftc.gov/opa/2009/10/endortest.shtm. Ftc.gov (2013-06-27). Retrieved on 2013-09-19.

[45] Alexandra Wharton (March/April 2007), Learning Outside the Box http://mthink.com/article/learning-outside-box/, *Revenue Magazine*, Issue: March/April 2007, Page 58, link to online version retrieved June 26, 2007

[46] Shawn Collins (June 9, 2007), Affiliate Millions - Book Report http://blog.affiliatetip.com/archives/affiliate-millions-book-report/, *AffiliateTip Blog*, retrieved June 26, 2007

[47] March/April 2007, How Do Companies Train Affiliate Managers? http://www.revenuetoday.com/story/webextra-issue16-2 (Web Extra), *RevenueToday.com*, retrieved June 26, 2007

[48] Vinny Lingham (11.October, 2005), Profit Sharing - The Performance Marketing Model of the Future http://www.vinnylingham.com/2006/10/special-report-profit-sharing-the-performance-marketing-model-of-the-future.html ,*Vinny Lingham's Blog*, retrieved on 14.May, 2007

[49] Linda Rosencrance, 15 April 2008, N.Y. to tax goods bought on Amazon http://www.computerworld.com/action/article.do?command=viewArticleBasic&taxonomyName=government&articleId=9077963&taxonomyId=13&intsrc=kc_top , *Computerworld*, retrieved on 16.April, 2008

[50] IAB, Friday, 27 March 2009 IAB affiliate council strengthens voucher code guidelines http://www.iabuk.net/en/1/iabaffiliatemarketingcouncilstrengthensonlinevouchercodebestpracticeguidelines270309.mxs

[51] https://dmoztools.net/Business/Opportunities/Online_Opportunities/Affiliate_Programs

[52] http://botw.org/top/Computers/Internet/Web_Design_and_Development/Authoring/Webmaster_Resources/Affiliate_Programs/

[53] //en.wikipedia.org/w/index.php?title=Template:Internet_marketing&action=edit

[54] Robinson et al. (2007) 'Marketing communications using digital media channels', in Chaffey, D. and Chadwick, F. E. (2016) Digital Marketing: Strategy, Implementation, and Practice.Edinburgh Gate: Pearson Education Limited, pp. 515-522.

[55] Albans, S. (2017) 'ASOS plc interim results for six months'. Available at: https://www.asosplc.com/~/media/Files/A/Asos-V2/results-archive/statement/interim-results-statement-04-04-2017.pdf. Retrieved 2017-05-11.

[56] //en.wikipedia.org/w/index.php?title=Template:Internet_marketing&action=edit

[57] Pew Internet & American Life Project, "Tracking surveys" http://www.pewinternet.org/trends.asp, March 2000 – March 2009

[58] How Scheduling Affects Rates http://www.mailermailer.com/resources/metrics/2012/how-scheduling-affects-rates.rwp. Mailermailer.com (July 2012). Retrieved on July 28, 2013.

[59] BtoB Magazine, "Early Email Blasts Results in Higher Click & Open Rates" http://www.btobonline.com/article/20110901/EMAIL13/309019997/early-morning-email-blasts-pay-off-with-strong-opens-clicks , September 2011

[60] UK e-mail marketing predicted to rise 15% http://www.mediaweek.co.uk/article/945161/uk-e-mail-marketing-predicted-rise-15. MediaWeek.co.uk (13 October 2009)

[61] "Why Email Marketing is King". Harvard Business Review (21 August 2012) http://blogs.hbr.org/2012/08/why-email-marketing-is-king/

[62] Roberts, A. "Email deliverability is on the decline: report", ClickZ https://www.clickz.com/email-deliverability-is-on-the-decline-report/104466/

[63] Fairhead, N. (2003) "All hail the brave new world of permission marketing via email" (Media 16, August 2003)

[64] O'Brian J. & Montazemia, A. (2004) Management Information Systems (Canada: McGraw-Hill Ryerson Ltd.)

[65] The Privacy and Electronic Communications (EC Directive) Regulations 2003 http://www.opsi.gov.uk/si/si2003/20032426.htm . Opsi.gov.uk. Retrieved on July 28, 2013.

[66] //en.wikipedia.org/w/index.php?title=Template:Internet_marketing&action=edit

[67] SearchEngineLand http://searchengineland.com/iab-search-was-50-of-digital-ads-219588

[68] https://www.google.com/webmasters/tools/mobile-friendly/

[69] Boughton, S. B. (2005). Search engine marketing. Perspectives in business, 20(4), 195-202.

[70] Boughton, S. B. (2005). Search engine marketing. Perspectives in business, 20(4), 195-202.

[71] Sen, R. (2005). Optimal search engine marketing strategy. International Journal of Electronic Commerce, 10(1), 9-25.

[72] Skiera, B., Eckert, J., & Hinz, O. (2010). An analysis of the importance of the long tail in search engine marketing. Electronic Commerce Research and Applications, 9(6), 488-494.

[73] David O. Klein & Joshua R. Wueller, Trademark Enforcement and Internet Search Advertising: A Regulatory Risk for Brand Owners http://papers.ssrn.com/abstract=2897528, IP Litigator, Nov./Dec. 2016.

[74] How Social Media Is Changing Paid, Earned & Owned Media http://mashable.com/2011/06/23/paid-earned-owned-media/. Mashable.com (2011-06-23). Retrieved on 2013-07-28.

[75] Zhang, M., Jansen, B. J., and Chowdhury, A. (2011) Influence of Business Engagement on Online Word-of-mouth Communication on Twitter: A Path Analysis https://faculty.ist.psu.edu/jjansen/academic/jansen_business_twitter.pdf. Electronic Markets: The International Journal on Networked Business. 21(3), 161-175.

[76] Bowden, J. (March 17, 2014). The Impact of Social Media Marketing Trends on Digital Marketing http://www.socialmediatoday.com/content/impact-social-media-marketing-trends-digital-marketing. socialmediatoday.com

[77] Gillin, P. (2007): The New Influencers, a Marketer's Guide to the new Social Media, Sanger, CA.

[78] Willis, Derek (2014-09-26) Narendra Modi, the Social Media Politician https://www.nytimes.com/2014/09/26/upshot/narendra-modi-the-social-media-politician.html?_r=0&abt=0002&abg=0. *New York Times*

[79] Schaffer, Neal. Maximize Your Social : A One-Stop Guide to Building a Social Media Strategy for Marketing and Business Success. Somerset, NJ, USA: John Wiley & Sons, 2013. ProQuest ebrary. Web. 3 December 2014. Copyright © 2013. John Wiley & Sons. All rights reserved.

[80] http://www.adweek.com/socialtimes/survey-96-of-recruiters-use-social-media-to-find-high-quality-candidates/627040

[81] http://www.business2community.com/infographics/impact-online-reviews-customers-buying-decisions-infographic-01280945#WHA7GjedRY1ami50.97

[82] Cassinelli, A. (2013-12-31). 13 Best Social Media Campaigns of 2013 http://www.postano.com/blog/13-best-social-media-campaigns-of-2013. *Postano*

[83] "About Twitter" https://about.twitter.com/, "Twitter", Retrieved on 27 June 2014.

[84] Caravella, Andrew. " Four Functions of Social Media Guide http://downloads.sproutsocial.com/Sprout-2013-Four-Functions-Guide.pdf." Retrieved 15 August 2013.

[85] https://www.whatsapp.com/about/ltitle=About Whatsapp

[86] https://www.whatsapp.com/features/ltitle=Features

[87] Lunden, Ingrid (2014-01-11) Ad 'Experiments' Come To Delicious As It Updates Social Bookmarking API With Authentication, Rate Limits https://techcrunch.com/2014/01/11/delicious-api-advertising/. techcrunch.com

[88] Aaron, Jesse (2014-06-18) "How to Integrate Reddit Into Your Next Digital Marketing Campaign" https://www.theguardian.com/media-network/media-network-blog/2014/jun/18/integrate-reddit-digital-marketing. *The Guardian*

[89] Parr, Benn (2009-08-06) "Digg Ads Are Here: Will Users Bury Them Into Oblivion?" http://mashable.com/2009/08/06/digg-ads-2 mashable.com

[90] Kotler, P., Burton, S., Deans, K., Brown, L., & Armstrong, G. (2013). marketing (9th ed.). NSW, Australia: Pearson Australia

[91] Fill, C., Hughes, G., & De Francesco, S. (2013). Advertising Strategy, creativity and media. London, UK: Pearson.

[92] Kotler, P., Burton, S., Deans, K., Brown, L., & Armstrong, G. (2013). marketing (9th ed.). NSW, Australia: Pearson Australia.

[93] Dahlen, M., Lange, F., & Smith, T. (2010). Marketing communications: A brand narrative approach. West Sussex, UK: John Wiley & Sons.

[94] Brito, M. (2013). How content governance will facilitate media company transformation. In Your brand (pp. 3-7). Retrieved from http://www.quepublishing.com/articles/article.aspx?p=2143149&seqNum=3

[95] Deshpande, P. (2014, August 24). The content marketing pyramid: Create more with less. Retrieved April 1, 2016, from http://contentmarketinginstitute.com

[96] Internet overtakes television to become biggest advertising sector in the UK https://www.theguardian.com/media/2009/sep/30/internet-biggest-uk-advertising-sector. *The Guardian* (2009-09-30)

[97] Twitter account dedicated to poke fun at Kenneth Cole for #Cairo tweet http//www.ibtimes.com. Ibtimes.com (2011-02-04). Retrieved on 2013-01-11.

[98] Kenneth Cole's Twitter Fail – PRNewser http://www.mediabistro.com/prnewser/kenneth-coles-twitter-fail_b14367. Mediabistro.com (2011-02-03). Retrieved on 2013-01-11.

[99] Wasserman, T. (2012-10-31). Gap Criticized For Insensitive Tweet During Hurricane Sandy http://mashable.com/2012/10/31/gap-tweet-hurricane-sandy/. mashable.com

[100] High price to be paid for controversial social-media mishaps http://www.sfgate.com/cgi-bin/article.cgi?f=/c/a/2011/03/16/BUA61ID19P.DTL *San Francisco Chronicle* March 17, 2011, retrieved April 4, 2012

[101] 領匯「尋味」腰斬 如何拆網絡炸彈 (The Link terminates its search for "old tastes": How to improve online corporate image http://lifestyle.etnet.com.hk/column/index.php/management/executive/10010?locdes=content, *Hong Kong Economic Times* April 20, 2012, retrieved April 25, 2012

[102] //tools.wmflabs.org/ftl/cgi-bin/ftl?st=wp&su=Social+media+marketing&library=OLBP

[103] //tools.wmflabs.org/ftl/cgi-bin/ftl?st=wp&su=Social+media+marketing

[104] //tools.wmflabs.org/ftl/cgi-bin/ftl?st=wp&su=Social+media+marketing&library=0CHOOSE0

[105] http://lib.dr.iastate.edu/etd/10447/

[106] "84.1% of US internet users view web video" http://www.broadbandtvnews.com/2010/11/15/84-1-of-us-internet-audience-viewed-online-video/, *Broadband TV News*, 15 November 2010.

[107] http://www.iab.net/media/file/IAB-Video-Ad-Format-Standards.pdf

Article Sources and Contributors

The sources listed for each article provide more detailed licensing information including the copyright status, the copyright owner, and the license conditions.

Digital marketing *Source:* https://en.wikipedia.org/w/index.php?oldid=803854288 *License:* Creative Commons Attribution-Share Alike 3.0 *Contributors:* ADbecks, AManWithNoPlan, Adtwiki, Ajayagarwal041, Ajaysonkusare, Alex Stepman, Alyseld, Anarchyte, Anilasnora, Apparition11, Archana1977, Aselshikh, Atulindian, Barek, Becktea, Bender235, Bephrem, Bgwhite, BillSiarkas, Bonadea, BronHiggs, Brownpaperbaguk, Businessappline, C2ashish, CAPTAIN RAJU, Cacuocbongda, ChrisLeeVella, Clubjustin, ClueBot NG, Codyeric, Cordless Larry, Crystalgames1, DRAGON BOOSTER, Darsanchallo, Datbubblegumdoe, David Biddulph, David.moreno72, Dcirovic, Deannew, Deli nk, Digital mania, DigitalVidya, Digitalever, Drpickem, Duvarag36, Euclidthalis, Eugene Wood, Everberne, Ewen, Expertfame, Falcon Kirtaran, Garimavardhan, Gilliam, Gogo Dodo, GoingBatty, Gossamers, Guillermo Cuadra, GünniX, Hazunda203, Himabindu123, I dream of horses, Iridescent, Jadertor, Jarble, John "Hannibal" Smith, Johnuniq, JoseRolles, Judasane, Junior5a, KBH96, KH-1, Kali lightworker888, Karthick Manickam, Kku, Kuru, LabFortyOne, Lankiveil, Lenavati, LeoFrank, LilHelpa, Lotje, MER-C, Madagala harish, Marcocapelle, MarkDaddy, Markerannie, Masasuas483024, Materialscientist, Mayajaros, Mayasai, Mean as custard, Meatsgains, MelbourneStar, Metalduky54, Mhonika Bharathi, Miguelthanhtran, Mild Bill Hiccup, MisterRandomized, Mnpcs1223, Momoja16, MottyOsher, Mswathi857, Nairji, NeilN, Nibhu, NickBailey94, Nicola1520, Nithinkoshy, Nk.tyagi44, Nmoshi, Ohnoitsjamie, PRADDYOT, Paticress, Pinkbeast, Prachetabim, RichardWeiss, Rifatka, Rjwilmsi, RunnyAmiga, Sabri.w, Sam.Dxn, Sami4ev3r, SandraHanaM, Sanket Edits Wiki, Sanya3, Satyam maddeshiya, Seosak, Shajeeh-ul-Hassan, Shopnito, Sirius Khan, Skdwived, Smalljim, Smartsocialbrand, Standar223, Stesmo, Storalora, Sunilkumar069, Sunnysinha123, Sunpower1, Sushant.iiml, Syncrotic, Theroadislong, Toankit, Top Social Marketing Solutions, Tortorj, Train2104, Tsindhu89, Versageek, Vickysks, Victuallers, Vivekanands28, Vivektomar1234, Vk lord, Volunteer1234, Wavelength, Wikingdynasty, Woodlot, WriterNeetin, YUVRAJ AHIRE, Yamont, Yasir196, Yostseo412, Zcarstvnz, 106 anonymous edits 1

Affiliate marketing *Source:* https://en.wikipedia.org/w/index.php?oldid=805602190 *License:* Creative Commons Attribution-Share Alike 3.0 *Contributors:* Abhay39, Adamghor, Ahsan5355, Amempire, Amsave, Ankit00923, Apparition11, BD2412, BEHeditor, Badaboum123, Barek, Bejnar, Bengteng172, Bgwhite, Bonadea, Bpruett72, Bretsdgrow, Brianmilner420, BronHiggs, Bshrair, CCespedes01, CLCStudent, Carllancaster, Carriedelvalle23, ChamithN, ChrisGualtieri, Clickbbd, ClueBot NG, Cnwilliams, Compfreak7, Countmolecular450BC, Cpamike, CyHack, DGG, DMacks, Dand96, Dannyruthe, Dawn Bard, Deli nk, DerHexer, Discospinster, Dyderik, Epicgenius, Eremit1977, Ericpet, Gabbarsingh07, GoingBatty, Grayfell, Hectic Ranking, IShadowed, Ireneshih, Jacbizer, Jalapenoface, Jatin kumar Hota, Jaypal24794, Johnuniq, Junioreditor, KH-1, Kahuta123, LKP1108, LisaK11, LondonPowellMarketing, Lone Crab Hand, Lugia2453, MCAWOOD, MER-C, Madalina Baroncea, MakeMoneys, Manpreet93, Marcmaxwell, Marketingjv, Markjohn22, Martinka1977, Materialscientist, Mauls, McGeddon, Mcawuk, Mean as custard, Mesbah098, Mikeblas, Mindmatrix, Mohammad9188, MrOllie, Narky Blert, NoAmCom, Numbermaniac, Ohnoitsjamie, Onel5969, PKT, Padenton, PaulMlumbo, Peter James, Peunet, Philip Trueman, Pratik8307, Purpleemu1, QuizzicalBee, Rahul SK Dubey, Razorflame, Redhotmustang, Rk tandon, Rodgers 15, Ronz, Rthelemaque, Ruhilgoyal, Ryangao, SEO Param Prakash, Samsara, Sandip.033, Seaphoto, Shahnawazsadique, Simonjon, Stesmo, Tadimeti111, TedFableZA, Terrylawson, Timesofpharma, Tomqj, Trappist the monk, Trivialist, Usmantariq4343, Versageek, Victor1249, Widr, Yamaguchi先生 , Zeeshanit512, Zellfaze, Zzuuzz, 140 anonymous edits 19

Display advertising *Source:* https://en.wikipedia.org/w/index.php?oldid=797823248 *License:* Creative Commons Attribution-Share Alike 3.0 *Contributors:* 88keysmedia, Alanasings, Amiodarone, Andy Dingley, Bamyers99, Barnstable1197, Beetstra, Boated idea s, Bruce1ee, CAPTAIN RAJU, ClueBot NG, Cumbrowski, David.moreno72, Deepikashanmathi, Distle, Download, Eduwebads, Excitingwhurray, Felosele, Frankstericio, Gamage wickramasiri, Gilliam, Ginevraruosi, Gmazeroff, Grandcaterers, Happysailor, Headbomb, HelenOnline, JLaTondre, JamesBWatson, Jeorgeaji, Jewelraz, Jim1138, Jwojdylo, K.dayan, KH-1, Keith D, Kevfav, KylieTastic, Lemnaminor, Liquidprinter, M. J. Joffe, Macrakis, Manosing293, Marcocapelle, Martushka12, Mdwh, Metalduky54, Michael randrup, MisfitToys, MrOllie, Myasuda, NYUPSER, Naren.bhanushali, Nyreader, Orangemike, Perf guru, Pinethicket, Princess Clown, Psharma1720, Qzd, Rajat.tyagii.tech, Raymond Sylvester, Rickburnes, Rjwilmsi, Rlquall, Robweatherhead, Rollins83, Ronz, Sarah.Nanasi, Sen Rorn, Sfan00 IMG, Sibisuren, Smtchahal, Solphusion∼enwiki, Stefanomione, Sunilpujee, Swliv, Tedder, TejasDiscipulus2, TheBlunderbuss, Theroadislong, Thesuites, Tigga, Tonysmith2014, Topbanana, TwoTwoHello, Vijay dlg vijay dlg, Waltloc, Widefox, Wikiuser905483, Willblieve, Woohookitty, Yanakorn.T, Yonil EVO, 88 anonymous edits 33

Email marketing *Source:* https://en.wikipedia.org/w/index.php?oldid=805431315 *License:* Creative Commons Attribution-Share Alike 3.0 *Contributors:* 331dot, 33emclarke, 65HCA7, Addisonharry7, Adeemjan666, AgnosticPreachersKid, Ahmadmorabeih, Aishsunshine, Akmela Priya, Akshayemail, Alex Stepman, AmandaEGagnon, Aparnarawal26, Arshadpanache, Arttechlaw, Asimhazro, AvalerionV, Back ache, Barek, Bbb23, BenWytt, Benespe, Bijun yang, Bilal-khan, Bimsreehari r, Bonadea, BorisBauerNYC, BradSquires, Brett-Aus, BronHiggs, Bsck1218, Chad.kiernan1, Chris.p2882, Chrishongkong, ClueBot NG, CostanzaK2, Cowlibob, CrystalC, Dai Pritchard, Dannyruthe, Dannyta91, Dawn Bard, Deli nk, Discospinster, Download, Dr. Blofeld, Drm310, Eddie at LeadFerret, Emailgenevieve, EsmeeNetwork, Estimi2, Excirial, Fachill, Felixrc91, Fraggle81, General Ization, Gilliam, Gladamas, Gogo Dodo, Greentree500, Hiuuf, HomeFinder1, IPUpfficia, Indeedawisechoice, Intgr, Iridescent, Irish79, Jacelcegan, Jackjomesaug, Jaewhi.lim, Jim1138, Jkbw, Jlenney, Jmccormac, John "Hannibal" Smith, Johnnyraug, Johnuniq, Kapil19pal, Kaur Pooja, Kcash03, Kku, Kpawan1, Krishnaraja sv, Kuru, Lightlowemon, LoganMcOwen, MBouch16, MER-C, Materialscientist, Maverickranger, Mayur tandon, McGeddon, Mdriyazalam, Me, Myself, and I are Here, Mean as custard, MelbourneStar, Metalduky54, Mild Bill Hiccup, Mohini8080, Mohitmunda, MrOllie, Mrjade312, Mswathi857, Murph9000, Nanishanbd, NeilN, Newpundit, Ngoc Minh Dao, Nihlus, Olga21, Outofcash, Perthite, Pidssdew, Pinkbeast, Preeti Sharma's Knowledge, R3esolution, Rajeshjhamb143, Rbeggy, Realtyfire, Rokmanrecords, RosePham, SARADIAZZ1, Shivanraptor, Soulparadox, SubSeven, Suomi viro, TechnologyFan, Terrylawson, Theroadislong, Timothy4321, Tothebeat.coo, Versageek, Victuallers, WP.ULTUGA, Waggie, Wakodeprashant6, Wiltzandrew, YatesByron, Zitchdog808, Zzuuzz, 125 anonymous edits 39

Search engine marketing *Source:* https://en.wikipedia.org/w/index.php?oldid=804136448 *License:* Creative Commons Attribution-Share Alike 3.0 *Contributors:* 40websolutions, 6it4pq, Agtx, Alex Stepman, Amiteb, Ammarpervez, Andrewstrass, Andy Dingley, Anirban.iitd, Ankit8492, Apparition11, Ashutosht2281, Atechnocrat01, Automatedsales, Bapbouvier, Barek, Bentogoa, Bharath.karthik15, Bhny, Bonadea, Bongwarrior, Brandylisa, Bri, BronHiggs, Bruce1ee, Cahk, Capitalismojo, Cari7942, ClueBot NG, Colonies Chris, CommonsDelinker, Cra20, DanaTodd, Darincarter, David.moreno72, Dawn Bard, Dcirovic, Deepkatiwari.xyz001, DefinitionWizard, Deli nk, DerBorg, Dewritech, Discospinster, Donner60, Dubseo1, ExtraBart, Fixer88, Foysal69, Gabbarsingh07, Gilliam, Gobonobo, GoddersUK, Goldencam, Hdt83, Integrityseo, Itslaxmikant, Jackfork, January, Jasonseoguy, Jblews, Jeraphine Gryphon, Jim1138, Jmccormac, JohnCD, Johnuniq, Jonesey95, JoseRolles, Jrw0212, Julietdeltalima, Juniorstrive, KH-1, Kaimu17, Karmaclub, KatalinG, Kp7777, Krano, Kuru, LOWCOSTSEOPLANS, Leavingacademia, Limon994, LisaG60, Loriwagoner, MBouch16, MER-C, Magioladitis, Manan.bhavsar9333, Maqs1231, MarkDowson, Markobravo7, Matt Edward, McGeddon, Me, Myself, and I are Here, Mean as custard, Metalduky54, Michael boyce, Michael.goldshmidt, MichaelWebMason, Mjblank, Morganglick, NadiaM3, NottNott, Onepalm, PrabhuBaskar, Prasanth5555, Psdab2016, Rajat.tyagii, Rajeevbadoni, Ramkinesan, RantorJakob, Raybrighton2016, Redbird is, Robertobarlow, Robinseed, Rohini Priya, Rrburke, Rsolar31g, RyanTylerThomas, SFK2, Samej82, Scarlettod, Seoatl, Seoblazedelhi, Seocompanyinhyd, Seosirohigulshan, Serols, Shahbaztamboli, ShawnSaver, Shiv Traders Scraps Buyers, Siddharthrj, Smtchahal, Steven Frederick Haines, Struggle99, Tassedethe, The Anonymouse, Thepinkfl, Theroadislong, Tiyasa.S, Tomwri, Transope, Trappist the monk, Trivialist, Unknown-pleasur, WUXIAOLIN, Widr, Wikpoint, YLoginov, Yintan, Zakpaklop, Zeradigital, Ziindia, ZioSolutions, Zzuuzz, 149 anonymous edits 45

Social media marketing *Source:* https://en.wikipedia.org/w/index.php?oldid=804674700 *License:* Creative Commons Attribution-Share Alike 3.0 *Contributors:* Akashghormode, Alex Stepman, Alexa Fox, Amiteb, Amortias, Anapalcic, Antonio Ramon80, Anuragggupta, Apparition11, BD2412, Barek, BenjaminJohnson, Bephrem, Bgwhite, Bonadea, Brett de Leijer, BrettofMoore, BronHiggs, Brussaa, CAPTAIN RAJU, Catlemur, Caydigitalgov, CerealKillerYum, ChrisOverton12, ClueBot NG, Crsisk, DRAGON BOOSTER, David.moreno72, Dcirovic, Deepakhmwiki, Deepblerg, Dewritech, Distle, Doyle Buehler, Duvarag36, Edwardglane, Electricmaster, Fachill, Favonian, Felixrc91, Fflmedia, Fixer88, Garimathakur20, General Ization, Giftlite, Giraffedata, GoingBatty, Grafen, Grayfell, Greentree500, Hannakay96, Headbomb, HelpUsStopSpam, Hramkumar108, I dream of horses, Irfansardar, Jasonmarlowe, Jimbob7770, Jubaer24, KBH96, KH-1, Kali lightworker888, Keblack777, Kinghoguie, Kirkvazquez, Kku, Km13oj, Kuru, Lazylaces, Leevan27, Leighvi, Lenavati, Liance, Libraryemilyr, LilHelpa, LillyW23, Lopifalko, Lwax314, MER-C, Macdonjo, Mackenziewalker, Magioladitis, Manoj Rawatz, Marcocapelle, Mariamitina1985, Materialscientist, McGeddon, Me, Myself, and I are Here, Mean as custard, Metalduky54, Mhonika Bharathi, Midigital, Mild Bill Hiccup, Mimpert, Mkmiriyala, Mleskanic, Mmcgarr, Mohtadimehran, MrOllie, MrX, Narky Blert, NeilN, Neils51, NiviKumar, Nyttend, Olgalira22, OnBeyondZebrax, Onel5969, Onyxxo, Optakeover, Oshwah, Pinkbeast, Pitalini, Prabhupanneerselvam92, Prachetabim, Pradeepiidt, Preethy Raghu, Pvtmahmoud, Quinto Simmaco, RA0808, Raffaele.filieri, RamonSilva80, Researcher9999, RickeyFeeds, Rituusingh, Rjwilmsi, Rk tandon, SJ Defender, Sakura Cartelet, Samiabdb, Sanmitra1, Saturn star, Seagull123, Serols, Shahzebraza, Snorre94, Sole arismendi, Sparkie82, Strikeescaperooms, Stuartmcclure, Subhalaxmi25, Susannewulf, Themogg, Theroadislong, Thetechchaser, Thomasdrapper, Usotw, Vijayaraghavan2910, Vladmedv, WayfaringWanderer, Wbm1058, WhySeoServices, Wiltzandrew, Wix 2016, WriterNeetin, Xurli, Yellowdesk, Znn6673, Виктор Јованоски, 84 anonymous edits 52

Video advertising *Source:* https://en.wikipedia.org/w/index.php?oldid=804995185 *License:* Creative Commons Attribution-Share Alike 3.0 *Contributors:* A.amitkumar, Bitstorm, Blethering Scot, Bonadea, Brycewilson7, ClueBot NG, Corn cheese, Din don, Distle, DonPrem, Eddietomalin, ElKevbo, Emma23 K, Factsearch, Froggygoo, Gilliam, Haeinous, Harikram, J. M., Jennica, Katharineamy, MER-C, Malcolma, Marcocapelle, Miyagawa, NiviKumar, Oshwah, Pinkbeast, RedMike-86-, RichardWeiss, Ronz, Rwalker, Serols, Solarra, The candide, Waggie, Waltloc, Wavelength, WillCoull, WillJoseph, Yoav.shai, YuvanshSharma, 37 anonymous edits 74

Image Sources, Licenses and Contributors

The sources listed for each image provide more detailed licensing information including the copyright status, the copyright owner, and the license conditions.

License

Index